KT-226-631

Decisions, decisions ...

Finding the will of God
in a complex world

Lawrence and Diana Osborn

Inter-Varsity Press

INTER-VARSITY PRESS
38 De Montfort Street, Leicester LE1 7GP, England

© Lawrence and Diana Osborn 1996

First published 1996

British Library Cataloguing in Publication Data
A catalogue record for this book is available from the British Library.

ISBN 0-85110-887-3

Set in Garamond

Typeset by Avocet, Brill, Aylesbury, Bucks
Printed in Great Britain by Cox & Wyman Ltd, Reading, Berkshire.

Inter-Varsity Press is the book-publishing division of the Universities and Colleges Christian Fellowship (formerly the Inter-Varsity Fellowship), a student movement linking Christian Unions in universities and colleges throughout the United Kingdom and the Republic of Ireland, and a member movement of the International Fellowship of Evangelical Students. For information about local and national activities write to UCCF, 38 De Montfort Street, Leicester LE1 7GP.

Contents

Introduction   7

1. The shepherd and his sheep   12

2. The foundations of guidance   30

3. The Bible and guidance   49

4. Know yourself   61

5. Circumstantial evidence   85

6. Be advised   107

7. Prayerful decision-making   124

8. Guidance and the community   141

9. When God is silent   157

10. No second best   175

Notes   186

Acknowledgments

We are grateful to all the friends who have shared their experiences of guidance with us during the preparation of this book, and to Canon Graham Kings who kindly permitted us to use his poem 'The Gospel of the Song'.

Introduction

Why guidance?

What is God's will for my life? What would God want me to do in these circumstances? How can I make the right choice?

At one time or another every Christian must ask himself or herself questions such as these. The desire to do God's will can be traced in the biographies and autobiographies of Christians of every era and culture.

However, in the modern era there seems to have been a peculiar emphasis on the mechanics and techniques of guidance. This contrasts sharply with the emphasis in earlier Christian thought and practice. The Reformers, such as Martin Luther and John Calvin, clearly expected God to guide believers. Calvin affirms the reality of God's guidance in his many sermons and writings, and yet he says remarkably little about how we actually receive his guidance.

Cultural pressures

Why has there been this shift in emphasis? We suspect that certain features of western culture have played an important part in shaping the contemporary Christian approach to divine guidance.

To begin with, we live in a culture for which the very idea of God has become problematic. The Christian view of God as a caring, transcendent Creator does not sit comfortably with western culture's vision of the universe as a self-sufficient mechanism. Cultural pressure to dismiss the voice of God as a delusion inevitably creates anxiety. How can I be certain that it is God speaking and not my own psyche?

In addressing that anxiety, the modern Christian is likely to be influenced by another aspect of western culture, namely its emphasis on technique. The unprecedented success of western technology inclines us to approach challenges as as-yet-unsolved problems, and to look for appropriate techniques to solve them. This obsession with technique extends even to our personal lives: much of the popular psychology industry consists of the packaging and sale of problem-solving techniques. The obsession is also visible within the church, where church-growth programmes harness secular techniques to enable clergy to manage their congregations more efficiently and sell their message more 'successfully'. And it influences our search for guidance. What is the best way of listening to God, and how can I best hear his voice?

A third factor that shapes our approach to God's

guidance is the hopelessness of our culture; it does not possess any ultimate meaning or goal. Without such a goal, hope is replaced by projects. Lacking any coherent vision of the future, we literally project our present into the future. The uncertainty of the future, however, continually threatens such narrowly conceived goals. As a result, our culture is obsessed with the need for security.

How is such security to be achieved? One of the basic slogans of modernity is 'Knowledge is power'. Applying that to the uncertainty of the future, we are encouraged to seek security in foreknowledge. Economic forecasting and futurology are widely employed to reduce these uncertainties. On a more popular level, many people in our supposedly scientific culture eagerly resort to pre-scientific techniques for anticipating and manipulating the future. Astrology, tarot cards and other forms of divination are more popular in the West today than they have been for centuries. In view of this cultural emphasis on security through foreknowledge, it is not surprising that the issue of divine guidance should be on the agenda of so many contemporary Christians.

Finally, the citizens of most modern western societies enjoy a degree of personal freedom that would have been unimaginable in most historical eras. In addition, our relative affluence affords us an unprecedented freedom of material choice. For example, the decisions associated with marriage create great anxiety for many Christians today. Is he or she the person God wants me to marry? If I miss God's will in this matter, won't I be condemning myself (and my spouse) to a second-class Christian life? But in many cultures, both in the past and today, such questions simply could not arise because most marriages are arranged. These questions are, at least in part, a product of the culture in which we live.

Theological confusion

To make matters worse, there is a tremendous amount of advice about seeking and doing God's will that is often contradictory.

For example, some people suggest that God has a detailed blueprint for every human life. Guidance for them is therefore about seeking God's unique will for at least some of the choices they have to make. Others put more stress on our God-given responsibility. For them, God is more like the conductor of a cosmic jazz orchestra: he controls the whole thing and ties it into one great work of art but, within that unity, he gives individuals considerable scope for improvisation. Furthermore, people who agree on this point may be divided over the actual means of guidance. Does God operate through Scripture and reason? Or may we expect direct inspiration by the Holy Spirit? Or does he operate through a variety of means?

These differences easily translate into confusion for us as we try to clarify our thinking on the issue. An inevitable result of such confusion is anxiety. Quite apart from whether this is the right thing to do, there is the anxiety over whether I have even gone about seeking God's will in the right way.

This is a book about the practice of seeking and doing God's will. However, given the level of confusion there appears to be in this area, we felt that any practical advice had to be set firmly in the context of basic theological principles. Before asking, 'How do I find the will of God for my life?' I must first ask, 'What is our God like, and what kinds of guidance would be consistent with his character as revealed in Scripture?' Then I must ask, 'What kind of creatures are we, and what kinds of guidance are appropriate, given that God has made us in this way?'

So the book begins by looking at what Scripture and Christian theology tell us about the character of God and human nature that might be relevant to discussion on guidance. Only then shall we embark on a discussion of the principles of guidance. The concluding chapters will look at various important issues relating to the application of those principles in the contemporary context.

One

The shepherd and his sheep

Guidance ... or a guide?

Imagine that you are enjoying a day out in the Scottish Highlands. You had an early start and the weather has been ideal. Now you realize that it is getting late and you have walked further than you had intended. You begin to make your way back to the car but even as you do so the weather changes. In a matter of minutes the cloudless skies are replaced by threatening storm clouds. It begins to rain and, because of the low clouds, you can no longer see clearly the way you have come. Soon you realize that it is beginning to get dark.

The clouds have closed in; night is falling; you are lost. If you are properly prepared, you will have a map and compass in your rucksack. However, they are of little use when the visibility is too poor to pick out any landmarks. What you need is the personal touch: an experienced guide with an intimate knowledge of these hills. If you are wise you will find some shelter, get out your survival blanket and wait for the mountain rescue team to come and get you.

We recently experienced a less life-threatening situation, when we took part in a parish weekend at Amport House near Andover. The organizers thoughtfully gave us a computer printout of directions to the conference centre. Unfortunately the last line of the directions read something like 'After 19 miles travelling west on the A303 take the *unknown* for 1 mile.' On a dark Friday evening this was easier said than done! Having consulted our own road atlas, we found the right exit. However, after about a mile we came to a T-junction. There were no signposts to show which way we should go and neither our directions nor our atlas could help us. We decided to turn left. That took us past the local pub where we stopped for personal directions: 'You should have turned right at the T-junction.'

As both these examples suggest, there is a deep difference between having guidance and having a guide.

Guidance can be impersonal. The guidebook and the DIY manual leave us in control. That is one of their attractions in a culture which places so much emphasis on individual freedom. Guidance gives us knowledge, and knowledge, according to our culture, is power. The only problem is that it leaves us to apply the knowledge ourselves. Without the ability to apply it, such knowledge is useless. A map of the mountainside is of little use if I do not know where I am, cannot see where I am going, or do not have a compass.

Furthermore, most of us rely on knowledge that

someone else has selected. Knowledge may be power but, if my knowledge is only partial, I am at the mercy of the person who has made the selection. Politicians may be economical with the truth. The media may slant the information they provide to favour commercial or political vested interests. The guidebook may omit interesting sites because of the bias or prejudice of the author. The person who relies on the computer manual will never really master the machine. In other words, while apparently offering us greater control, impersonal guidance may be highly manipulative.

On the other hand, a guide is personal. When we put ourselves in the hands of a guide, we are consciously surrendering control over an aspect of our lives. It requires an act of faith. We have to trust the guide – and show our trust by acting on his or her advice.

It should be immediately obvious that the image of a personal guide is more consistent with the witness of Scripture than that of impersonal guidance. That God cares for us is an explicit and recurring theme throughout Holy Scripture.

The Old Testament, in particular, repeatedly portrays *God as a shepherd* who tends and guides his people Israel. For example, Jeremiah promises that 'He who scattered Israel will gather them and will watch over his flock like a shepherd' (Jeremiah 31:10b). It is a communal image: a shepherd cares for an entire flock. But it is, none the less, personal. The shepherd cares for the flock precisely by caring for every individual member. Jesus makes this clear in the parable of the lost sheep (Luke 15:3-7). So, when blessing Joseph, Jacob speaks of 'the God who has been my shepherd all my life to this day' (Genesis 48:15b). And, of course, in that most famous of psalms, David proclaims that 'The LORD is my shepherd' (Psalm 23:1). Significantly, it is also an image that Jesus used to describe himself (*e.g.* John 10:7, 11, 14), and subsequently it became one of his titles: the 'great Shepherd of the sheep' (Hebrews 13:20).

Another recurring biblical image relevant to the question of guidance is that of *God as our counsellor*. Again, thanks to the words of Isaiah, this has become a title of the Lord Jesus: he is 'Wonderful Counsellor' (Isaiah 9:6). This is striking because it contrasts sharply with our notions of God as King and Lord. A king commands but a counsellor advises. As Lord, God has the power to override our free will, but the image of the counsellor suggests that he does not do so. Rather, God is presented as the giver of good advice. What we do with that advice is our responsibility.

The Bible also makes it clear that God cares for us as individuals. For example, Jesus tells the disciples, 'Are not two sparrows sold for a penny? Yet not one of them will fall to the ground apart from the will of your Father ... so don't be afraid; you are worth more than many sparrows' (Matthew 10:29, 31). If God's care extends to individual sparrows, we may rest assured that it encompasses individual human beings! But does this care extend to the giving of individual guidance when we ask it of him?

Again the Bible is full of promises that such guidance is available to all who seek it. God 'guides the humble in what is right' (Psalm 25:9a). He promises through the psalmist, 'I will instruct you and teach you in the way you should go; I will counsel you and watch over you' (Psalm 32:8), while the prophet asserts, 'The LORD will guide you always; he will satisfy your needs in a sun-scorched land' (Isaiah 58:11a). That Paul expected God to guide is apparent from his prayer for the Colossian Christians, that God might fill them with 'the knowledge of his will through all spiritual wisdom and understanding' (Colossians 1:9).

God promises to guide us because of who he is, not because of who or what we are. Guidance is not dependent upon particular holiness or knowledge of the right techniques. It is not a matter of reading the right books (after all, many generations of Christians have managed great things for God without the 'benefit' of the current massive literature on the subject!). No, God guides us because he loves us.

Implicit in the scriptural promises of divine guidance is the assumption that God is able and willing to communicate with us. This is an important point to bear in mind when considering the question of divine guidance. Dallas Willard warns:

> It is possible to talk about conscious guidance in terms of mysterious feelings, curious circumstances, and special scriptural nuances of meaning to the point where God's very character is called into question. He is not a mumbling trickster.[1]

On the contrary, Scripture testifies that God is perfectly able to communicate precisely what he wants to communicate. If he needs us to know

16

something, we may rest assured that he will get the message across.

The people God guides

God guides people because he loves them. He created us in his image so that we might live in personal relationship with him. This is fundamental to the Christian understanding of human nature, and it also has important implications for the nature of guidance.

Perhaps the most important aspect of being created in the image of God is the fact of *human freedom*. One thing is certain: the God of the Bible is free; and we are his images. God demonstrates his freedom by creating, and significantly the biblical references to our being in the image of God generally appear in the context of creation or creativity (*e.g.* Genesis 1:26–27; Psalm 8:4–8). However, our capacity to be creative also implies a capacity to destroy. Because we are free, we are also responsible. So, we may expect God to treat us as (morally) responsible creatures. In other words, because of the kind of creatures God intends us to be, we may expect that he will not guide in a way that overrides or suppresses our freedom.

This is an important point. Too many enthusiastic believers seem to think that holiness means passivity. Someone once called this the 'Jesus-wants-me-for-a-cabbage' syndrome. The difference between passive submission and a genuine loving relationship is well illustrated by the film *The Stepford Wives*. In the film, a couple move into the middle-American town of Stepford. At first it seems idyllic: the husbands go out to work and their wives care for their homes. But, gradually, the heroine becomes suspicious of the fulfilment other women seem to get out of domestic chores. They never fight; they have no opinions of their own; their lives revolve around the task of making their husbands as comfortable as possible. Of course there are exceptions, but they tend to go on holiday and return just like the rest. Too late the heroine realizes that the human wives are systematically being replaced by robotic copies! The robots were mechanical slaves, dedicated to pleasing their male owners but incapable of being their friends. The point is simple: genuine personal relationships do not thrive upon the mindless conformity of one of the parties – and neither does our relationship with God.

Another important aspect of being created in the image of God is that, just as God is self-giving, we were *created to be self-giving*. According to Genesis, God created us with a mission: to have dominion over the earth; to be his agents in governing the earth. Contrary to modern misinterpretations, this was not a *carte blanche* to exploit creation. Rather, it was a call to care for the earth. It was (and is) a position of responsible service.

Dominion is a position of service rather than domination because it has to be understood in the light of Christ's lordship. We are servants, not so much because we acknowledge Christ's lordship over our lives (though we do) but because Christ elevates us to share in his lordship.

Jesus called them together and said, 'You know that those who are regarded as rulers of the Gentiles lord it over them, and their high officials exercise authority over them. Not so with you. Instead, whoever wants to become great among you must be your servant, and whoever wants to be first must be slave of all. For even the Son of Man did not come to be served, but to serve, and to give his life as a ransom for many' (Mark 10:42–45).

A dominion that bears the distinguishing marks of Christ's lordship will be an existence of freely chosen service.

This characteristic of Christian existence suggests something else about guidance. When we seek God's will, we are likely to find ourselves being guided in the way of service. Guidance is likely to be other-centred, encouraging that overflow of generosity which builds up towards Christian maturity.

The New Testament adds an important new dimension to our understanding of human freedom. In order to enter into the privileges and responsibilities intended for us by God, we must first be set free. The heart of the gospel is the truth that Jesus Christ has set us free. He has liberated us from the power of sin and death.

The positive aspect of Christian freedom is regularly expressed in the pages of the New Testament by the concept of adoption. We were slaves. Jesus Christ has set us free. However, he has not merely cut through one set of ties that bound us to an ultimately destructive way of living. He has also established another set of relationships. By his actions, he has made us part of the family of God.

If we are God's adopted children, God's care for us is that of a father. It is far more intimate than we might imagine from the pictures of him as our shepherd and counsellor. Because God is our Father, we can ask for guidance or advice and expect a reply. And just as an earthly father's guidance might involve discipline, we are told that 'the Lord disciplines those he loves, and he punishes everyone he accepts as a son' (Hebrews 12:6). This is not punishment for punishment's sake, but training to bring us to maturity. Our Father's advice will always be designed to help us become more mature. So we may not expect him simply to make our decisions for us. Asking God for guidance should never be confused with asking him to take responsibility away from us.

The goal of maturity brings us to a final image for the kind of people God guides: 'friends of God'. The goal of adoption is to have children who are capable of inheriting. God does not want children who remain immature. He wants his children to become responsible Christlike adults.

As children grow up, so their relationship with their parents changes. It becomes no longer appropriate for the parents to tell them what time to go to bed or remind them to wash behind their ears. The goal of responsible parenthood is to bring up children who can make sensible decisions about much larger matters than these. As parents we hope that our advice and example over the years will encourage our grown children to confide in us and, when appropriate, to seek our advice. But we do not particularly want to be burdened with making their decisions for them. In other words, we hope that the relationship will change from one of dependence to one of friendship.

Similarly, God's goal in adopting us as his children is that we grow into Christlike maturity. As we grow towards this goal, we do not cease to be his children but we become his friends. In terms of guidance and decision-making, this implies a movement towards greater freedom to make important decisions for ourselves. Of course, this does not mean that we will stop seeking the advice and help of God; quite the opposite. Responsible decision-making involves the maturity to be able to take advice from others. However, it also means recognizing that the decision is ours to make. Maturity in decision-making implies that we do not use requests for advice to evade the responsibility of deciding for ourselves. Finally, responsibility in decision-making does not necessarily imply that we will make the right decision. Rather, it means that we are prepared to take full responsibility for all our choices, including our wrong choices.

Guidance and God's purposes

The God we worship is the Creator of the universe. As we have already noted, this was the ultimate act of divine freedom: God chose to create. It was not something imposed upon him. Neither was it an arbitrary demonstration of divine power. The Bible makes it clear that God has a purpose in creation and, in order to fulfil that purpose, has maintained an active guiding interest in its every aspect.

Does this mean that God has *a detailed blueprint* for creation? Not necessarily. The view that God specifically wills every minute detail of the universe only makes sense in a particular context. It is a way of reconciling the closed mechanical universe of classical physics with the traditional view of God as sovereign and active. It is true, we have a God who painstakingly maps out every detail of creation beforehand. Jesus presented us with a God who knows and cares about the life and death of every sparrow. The blueprint view of divine providence goes much further: God consciously ordains every change of state of every subatomic particle.

Applying this to guidance leads to the notion of an individual will of God for each believer; the belief that God has a detailed blueprint for our lives, which encompasses every decision we ever make.

This belief poses serious problems for human freedom. Some Christians have such a high view of God's sovereignty that they cannot envisage anything which God has not already foreordained. For example, Garry Friesen asks:

> Would you like to know His sovereign plan for the past? Find a good history book and curl up with it on a rainy day. If something happened, it was part of the plan.[2]

This implies that whatever will happen in the future is also part of the plan. God has already anticipated whatever decisions I make. They are already part of the plan. Such a view of God's sovereignty may give us a sense of security, but it does so at the expense of our freedom.

This can lead to the will of God being treated as a synonym for fate: what will be, will be. God is working his purpose out and it is not my place to interfere. My job is to carry on obediently in the sphere of life to which God has called me. Such an excessive view of God's sovereignty discourages me from taking the initiative. By playing down my freedom, it undermines my responsibility.

This modern image of God as a cosmic planner is very different from the older model of God as king of the universe. To say that God is King is to say that he has ultimate authority. Given the biblical concepts of kingship, it also suggests that God cares for his creatures as a king cares for his subjects.

However, a king does not attend to every detail in person. On the contrary, a king is one who can act precisely by commanding others. A king uses agents: he has courtiers and servants. That God works through secondary agents is a recurring theme in traditional theology. For example, in discussing God's blessings, Calvin insists that when we give thanks to God we should not forget also to thank the human agents through whom those blessings have come.

Action of this kind does not require a detailed blueprint. A possible analogy might be that of the military commander. Generals do not usually concern themselves with the details of a battle. They concentrate on strategy, on the overall plan, and delegate the details to their lieutenants.

The biblical image of God as our shepherd also

supports this. A shepherd does not completely determine the activity of his sheep. Rather, he leads the flock to good pasture and determines safe limits for its movements. Each sheep is free to move about within those limits. Similarly, we may see much of God's guidance as the setting of safe limits for our freedom.

God has *an overall plan*. The doctrine of divine sovereignty affirms that nothing can thwart God's purposes for creation. In the end, God will triumph. Ultimately, resisting the will of God is comparable to King Canute's attempts to command the tide.

The view that God has an overall plan does not require us to believe that God works out every detail with mechanical precision. The sovereignty of God suggests that he has a strategy for the fulfilment of his purposes in creation. Far from denying human freedom, that strategy encompasses it. So God can allow acts which run counter to his will and transform them to facilitate his purposes. Take, for example, Joseph's brothers in the Old Testament. Their action in selling Joseph as a slave was intentionally evil. But God overrode their evil intent and brought about a quite unexpected outcome. As Joseph himself says at the end of the story: 'You intended to harm me, but God intended it for good to accomplish what is now being done, the saving of many lives' (Genesis 50:20).

God's plan for creation is one that takes into account human freedom. Indeed, according to traditional theology, God's sovereignty guarantees human freedom. God gives us room for manoeuvre. In this respect he is more like the master builders who designed the great medieval cathedrals than like modern architects. One of the beauties of the great cathedrals is that much of the ornamentation was left to the discretion of the individual craftsmen. God gives us ample opportunity to make responsible decisions that he can then weave into the cosmic tapestry.

The character of God and the nature of guidance

Our images of God inevitably shape our expectations of guidance. False images will distort our expectations of guidance accordingly. In concluding this chapter, it may be helpful to summarize what we can expect from God as we have so far described him.

To begin with, the guidance we may expect from God will be shaped by God's character. A recurring theme of the Bible is God's faithfulness. He does not change or contradict himself. Therefore we may be certain that any guidance we receive will be consistent with what Scripture has revealed of God's character.

An important aspect of God's character is his righteousness. According to Psalm 23, God guides 'in paths of righteousness'. God will never guide us to steal, lie or commit murder. Any guidance we receive will conform to the standards of morality revealed in the Bible.

Another dimension of God's character on which Scripture dwells is his wisdom. Underpinning God's will and capacity for action is wisdom. So his will is never arbitrary.

Hannah Whitall Smith recounts a woman who used to seek God's guidance even about what clothes to wear:

> As she put on each article she asked the Lord whether she was to put it on, and very often the Lord would tell her to put on the right shoe and leave off the other; sometimes she was to put on both stockings and no shoes; and sometimes both shoes and no stockings; it was the same with all the articles of dress ...[3]

The sheer arbitrariness of what the woman took to be God's leading is a clear indication that all was not right.

A personal God who seeks a personal relationship with us will prefer modes of guidance that are personal rather than mechanical. Practices such as astrology, geomancy and the use of tarot cards for the purposes of divination are impersonal, mechanical ways of attaining insight. Quite apart from their occult associations, they are not legitimate Christian practices simply because they are so impersonal and mechanical.

The Bible may lend little support to the idea of a divine cosmic blueprint but it does reveal God as a loving Father who is intimately concerned with every aspect of our lives. The Bible clearly teaches that God relates to us as unique persons. We can have a personal relationship with God: we are offered membership of God's family; we are offered friendship with God. We may therefore expect God to guide us personally.

26

Such guidance can be very specific without being a blueprint. For example, we know that specific words from God influenced Paul's missionary journeys on several occasions. On one occasion (Acts 16:7), the Spirit prevented Paul and his companions from preaching in Bithynia. Soon afterwards, Paul received a vision calling him to take the gospel to Macedonia. This is specific guidance but it lacks the detail of a blueprint.

Other New Testament accounts of divine guidance suggest that it is not coercive. God respects our freedom. He will certainly give advice but that advice is not necessarily conclusive. We may choose to ignore God's advice. Furthermore, there may be situations where it is not wrong for us to do so. Again, the life of the apostle Paul provides a good example: Paul has concluded that another visit to Jerusalem would most effectively further the cause of the gospel. He interprets this very deep desire to serve God, at whatever personal cost, as the compulsion of the Spirit (Acts 20:22). But what is God actually saying to him at this time? Paul freely confesses that God's consistent advice is that this journey will in fact end in his imprisonment (Acts 20:23; *cf.* 21:10–15). So is Paul wilfully ignoring God's will? Or is God testing his resolve? Surely the latter. But, if so, the implication is that this is Paul's free choice. Knowing the consequences (how could he not, since God has made them only too clear?), he nevertheless chooses for himself the course of action that, to the best of his knowledge, will most effectively promote God's kingdom.

This highlights another theme that has appeared more than once in the preceding discussions. We may expect God's guidance to be of a kind that will help us to grow as Christians. Here, it takes the form of a warning: if you do this for me, imprisonment will follow. Paul grows by freely choosing to do it despite the personal consequences.

We ask for guidance. But this characteristic of divine guidance implies that the advice we receive from God may not be what we want at all. Like a wise counsellor, God may be non-directive in his advice. He may choose not to tell us what to do precisely because, consciously or unconsciously, we are seeking his advice in order to evade our responsibilities. Sometimes our daughter asks us for help with her homework. We could simply tell her the answers. That would save us all much time and trouble! But it would also lead to an unhealthy dependence upon us. She has to learn to solve these problems for herself. So we begin by showing her how we would solve one or two of the problems; then we encourage her to try some more on her own. Gradually we withdraw our assistance while encouraging her to believe in her own abilities (and, perhaps, warning her of the pitfalls in particular cases).

Finally, we may expect any guidance that God gives us to be shaped by God's purposes. God is working ceaselessly towards the ultimate fulfilment of creation and, within that overall plan, he wants the best for each individual creature. Therefore we may expect God to give us whatever guidance we need in order to serve him effectively.

What God perceives as our need and what we may want in a given situation, however, are very different things. God's guidance may therefore not meet our expectations. God's fatherly care for us may be focused on issues other than where we should live, what we should do, whom we should marry and in which church we should worship. What seems so important from the perspective of Huntingdon on 20 May 1994, for example, may not have the same significance when seen in the light of eternity!

As we have already pointed out, God is interested in the development of mature responsible creatures who are capable of worshipping him freely. He will guide us with such purposes in view. And, if it better serves our growth in responsibility and maturity, he is free to withhold his guidance.

Two

The foundations of guidance

Having looked briefly at the character of the God who guides and the nature of the creatures whom he guides, it is time to turn to the question of guidance itself. We shall begin by exploring the attitudes we should adopt when seeking God's guidance.

Faithfulness

It is often suggested that expecting God to guide us is unreasonable if we are not already acting on advice previously received. After all, if someone asks our advice, dismisses it and yet asks again later, we may wonder what it is they really want. Some indication that we are likely to take such advice seriously is surely a prerequisite for continued guidance.

Obedience to what we already know of God's will is frequently presented as an essential foundation for guidance. In particular, we might be expected to be living according to the standards revealed in Scripture: practising holiness. Dallas Willard puts the challenge of holiness as a series of questions that are helpful in the task of self-examination:

> What am I doing in life that would make his speaking to me a reasonable thing for him to do? Are we in business together in life? Or am I in business just for myself, trying to 'use a little God' to advance my projects?[1]

The idea of obedience as a prerequisite for guidance, however, is open to misinterpretation. Given our culture's obsession with technique, I may be tempted to believe that my obedience gives me a certain leverage with God. Alternatively, I may wrongly equate obedience with mindless submission.

We prefer to speak of faithfulness rather than obedience as a foundation for guidance. Obedience may be nothing more than rule-keeping. Faithfulness has more positive connotations. It is my loving response to a loving God. It is my desire to please the one who has done so much and suffered so much for me. Moreover, it is a response that predisposes me to listen to my heavenly lover. Faithfulness is that attitude which continually asks, 'How can I please God in this situation?' It is a response that encourages me not to dwell too much on guidance but to look to the Guide. As Thomas à Kempis once wrote:

> The prudent lover does not so much consider the lover's gift as the love of the giver. He looks rather at the love than the value, and sets all that which is given below the beloved.[2]

Similarly with guidance: the fact of guidance is secondary to the love of our divine guide.

31

The basic expressions of faithfulness to Christ have not changed significantly in two thousand years.

'If you love me, you will obey what I command' (John 14:15), Jesus says to the disciples during the Last Supper. *Obedience* is necessary but, as we have already noted, not sufficient. It cannot be sufficient because it does not go to the heart of the matter. It is not mere obedience that God wants but faithfulness or love. Only the obedience that flows from love as its expression is acceptable to God.

Prayer is another essential part of our relationship with God. All personal relationships are built upon personal communication. A balanced prayer life will be more than the recitation of a shopping list. The ACTS formula (Adoration, Confession, Thanksgiving, Supplication) makes it clear that asking God for what we need is only a part of what it is to pray. Like any other intimate communication between lovers, prayer includes not only the expression of our desires but also saying sorry and appreciating the other person. One element missing from this formula is the silence in which we listen to the beloved: prayer, like other forms of conversation, should be a dialogue rather than a monologue.

This is the point at which the Bible comes in. At least part of the silence of prayer will be given over to prayerful *attention to Scripture*. Why? Because the Christian Bible, besides being a unique record of our spiritual forebears' encounters with God, is God's primary way of revealing himself to the world. If you like, the Scriptures are God's love letters to the human race.

An aspect of faithfulness that tends to be neglected in our individualistic culture is that of meeting with other Christians. According to Scripture, God did not design us to be isolated individuals. On the contrary he treats us as persons in community. *Communal worship and mutual support* are integral parts of the Christian life. The neglect of this aspect of Christian life has impoverished our experience of God's guidance. We tend not to seek the advice and support of the church in our personal decision-making. Yet it is clear from the New Testament that God can and does speak through the community (*e.g.* Acts 13:1–3). Recognizing this impoverishment, some strands of contemporary Christianity have sought to redress the balance only to fall into forms of communal decision-making that are not appropriate. Because of its contemporary importance, this aspect of guidance will be explored more fully in later chapters.

Actively seeking the kingdom

Working for the kingdom of God and actively serving its interests is the pro-active dimension of Christian faithfulness. One of the most memorable lines from the Sermon on the Mount must surely be, 'But seek first his kingdom and his righteousness, and all these things will be given to you as well' (Matthew 6:33). Jesus was referring primarily to tangible things, the necessities of life, but he was also addressing his hearers' anxieties about the future: 'Therefore do not worry about tomorrow …' (Matthew 6:34a).

Part of our desire for guidance grows from similar

anxieties. To that part Jesus effectively says, 'Don't worry about it. Put the kingdom first. Follow me.'

However, another and more important part of our desire for guidance is born precisely from that command to seek first the kingdom. What does this mean for us in practical terms? How are we to seek the kingdom in our homes and workplaces?

Many environmental activists attempt to live by the slogan, 'Think globally, act locally.' It is a useful slogan, and may be paraphrased to express what is meant by seeking the kingdom. To seek God's kingdom we must 'serve locally and think globally'.

The desire to please our beloved (which should be a fundamental part of the Christian faith) will spur us to look out for small opportunities to serve him locally. Christian service is marked by humility (*i.e.* it is 'down to earth' rather than self-effacing).

After Jesus healed him, the man who had been called Legion wanted to follow him. Yet Jesus said, 'Go home to your family and tell them how much the Lord has done for you, and how he has had mercy on you' (Mark 5:19). This was not a rejection; it was a vocation. Jesus was, in effect, saying, 'You can serve me best by serving me at home.'

Similarly, Paul insists, 'Each one should remain in the situation which he was in when God called him' (1 Corinthians 7:20; *cf.* 7:17, 24). God usually calls us to serve him where we already are. Christian service is not an exercise in romantic escapism.

Serving God locally, seeking his kingdom in our homes and workplaces and neighbourhoods, requires us to be on the look-out for any opportunities, however small. It may not be self-effacing, but neither does it stand on its dignity. If we perceive something as an opportunity to serve God, we should not ignore it because we are waiting for some larger sphere of service more acceptable to our pride and dignity. The way of seeking the kingdom locally is the way of the servant depicted so graphically by Jesus when he washed the disciples' feet (John 13:1-15).

However, seeking the kingdom is more than being open to local opportunities for service. An awareness of the bigger picture must always balance local service. The kingdom of which we are the servants is universal in its scope.

While accepting the local opportunities that present themselves, we should also be actively seeking bigger opportunities to serve God. Here we must beware of looking with the eyes of the secular world. The larger sphere to which God is calling us may be invisible to non-Christians. Conversely, those spheres of activity that are visibly 'successful' may be of less significance to God. We are tempted to regard the Christian leader with an over-full diary as 'more important' than a humble, retired member of the congregation who can do little but sit at home and pray. God may very well see things differently. While learning to think globally for the kingdom, we must be learning to see the world the way God sees it.

This dual process of serving locally and thinking globally is a prerequisite for divine guidance. It is so because it is one positive expression of our faithfulness. In addition, God's guidance is directed towards the coming of the kingdom in its fullness.

Those who are seeking first the kingdom, who are willing God's will, are more inclined to hear and act on such guidance.

Listening for God's guidance is therefore not simply a passive thing. It is something we engage in actively. We prepare ourselves for the larger call by serving locally, and thinking globally makes us aware of the wider opportunities. An outstanding example of this is that great missionary pioneer of the nineteenth century, Hudson Taylor. A burning passion to preach the gospel to the Chinese dominated his life. However, that very powerful vocation did not make him withdraw from other less romantic forms of Christian service. For example, when studying medicine, he could have argued that this was important preparatory work which should take priority over other forms of Christian service. Instead, he continued to preach, and was a tireless visitor of the sick and the poor. As for thinking globally, his passion for China had not come out of the blue. Rather, it was formed by a family tradition of informed prayer for world mission in general and the needs of China in particular.

Taking risks for the kingdom

Seeking first the kingdom is the pro-active dimension of faithfulness. It is therefore not just about responding to opportunities, large or small, near or far, as they present themselves, but also about creating such opportunities.

The idea that we should be taking risks for the sake

of the kingdom seems alien to us. However, it is a clear element of one of the most famous parables of the kingdom, the parable of the talents. There, God is portrayed as an absentee landlord and we are likened to servants left with the responsibility of managing his household and protecting his interests until his return. Each servant is entrusted with a certain sum of money. The faithful servants are those who 'put his money to work' (Matthew 25:16). He gave them no explicit instructions, but they looked for opportunities and were prepared to take risks to further their master's interests. By contrast, the one who plays it safe, who will not even risk his master's money to the bankers, is condemned as wicked and lazy.

The faithful servants did not need explicit instructions. They loved their master and desired to do whatever they could to improve and extend what he had entrusted to them. They had internalized their master's will. They freely willed his will.

This should be our aim in relation to the will of God. Many commentators on the Lord's Prayer have made this point about the petition, 'Your will be done on earth as in heaven.' It cannot be an abstract petition. We cannot pray 'your will be done' unless we accept the unspoken qualification 'beginning with me'. Whatever else it may be, this petition is a request that God so transform our wills that we freely choose his will. Accordingly, Calvin could say:

By this prayer we are formed to self-denial so God may rule us according to his decision ... and while the Spirit is inwardly teaching us we may learn to love the things that please him and to hate those which displease him. In consequence, our wish is that he may render futile and of no account whatever feelings are incompatible with his will.[3]

Willing God's will is not a matter of self-improvement. It is not something we can achieve on our own by dint of hard work or self-discipline. No, it is a matter for prayer and trust. We must ask God to transform our desires, feelings and will so that they conform to his will. And we must trust God to answer that prayer.

Moreover, we should not assume that, because we really want to do something, it cannot be God's will for us. The Victorian stiff-upper-lip attitude that says, 'If it hurts, it must be good for us', and conversely, 'If we enjoy it, it must be wrong', is a distortion of the truth. Far from denying our feelings and suppressing our desires, we should trust God to transform them in answer to our repeated petition, 'Your will be done.' We may expect that, as we grow in Christian maturity, we will increasingly want what God wants. However, even as young Christians we may will God's will. This is not to say that we should not examine our motives. But neither should we impute to God the entirely false character of a celestial killjoy.

The kind of love expressed in faithfulness is also the kind of love that casts out fear. We are prepared to take risks to please or to serve the one we love. Notice that the unfaithful servant was paralysed by fear. Such fear may push me into a false conservatism in which I refuse to listen to any message from God that might disturb my security. Alternatively, it may lead me into an infantile dependence in which I want God to decide for me. I turn the various means through which God advises me into oracles to be obeyed without question. Ironically, in such circumstances, God may withdraw his guiding activity to force me to take responsibility for my own actions. Either way, fear has effectively limited the guidance I am prepared to hear.

A dramatic example of someone who has taken risks for God's kingdom is Jackie Pullinger. She felt called to be a missionary but was turned down by all the societies to which she applied. In the end, she took the problem to a priest who knew her well. His advice was:

'Well, if you've tried all the conventional ways and missionary societies and God is still telling you to go, you had better get on the move.'

I felt frustrated.

'If you had a job, a ticket, accommodation, a sick fund and a pension, you wouldn't need to trust Him,' Richard continued. 'Anyone can go that way whether they are Christians or not. If I were you I would go out and buy a ticket for a boat going on the longest journey you can find and pray to know where to get off.'

I did not exactly hear bells but this was the first time in all those months of searching that anything made sense.

'It sounds terrific – but it must be cheating because I'd love to do that.' I still had the idea that anything to do with God had to be serious. I was sure that Christians always had to take the hard way and enjoyment was no part of suffering for their faith.[4]

The priest allayed her fears, however, and so, like Abraham, she set out with nothing more than her faith in God to guide her. The result is well known: a thriving ministry which has brought the light of Christ into the darkest corners of Hong Kong.

Listening expectantly

The unanimous teaching of biblical precedent, Christian history and traditional theology is that we can and should expect God to guide us. So another prerequisite for guidance is the expectation that God will guide. If we do not believe that God longs to guide us, then we may not hear him. Related to this is the question of how God communicates with us. We may expect God to guide but that will do us little good unless we have some expectations about how that guidance might come to us.

We communicate primarily through words. Similarly, we may expect God to communicate through words. We have already noted the importance of Scripture as the main verbal means through which God has communicated his will to the human race.

Another traditionally recognized way in which God may speak is through other people. The avenue of communication given most emphasis in Protestant theology is the sermon. This is (or ought to be) more than just the preacher's bright ideas about the Bible. The sermon is an opportunity for God to speak to his gathered people through (and sometimes in spite of) the words of the preacher.

In the Bible, God frequently speaks prophetically through the words (or actions) of some individual. Examples from church history suggest that we cannot rule out such prophetic words today. More mundane perhaps are those words of advice that are somehow so much more appropriate than the other person could possibly realize.

Since God is the power undergirding every creature, God can communicate through any human communication. Any written or spoken word has the potential to become God's word to us.

A particular case would be our own words. Ministers often comment that, when they preach, they find that they are preaching as much to themselves as to anyone else. Diana has certainly found this to be her own experience. Similarly, Lawrence has found the discipline of keeping a journal to be another way in which our own words may also be words that God addresses to us.

By extension, we may expect God to speak to us through our own inner voice. In a memorable phrase, the translators of the King James Version presented God as speaking to Elijah through a 'still small voice' (1 Kings 19:12). Is it the voice of conscience? The voice of our feelings? A voice from the subconscious? Our stream of consciousness itself? It is impossible to say. Nor does it really matter, since God, the Creator of our minds in both their conscious and unconscious aspects, could use any of these channels.

Western culture has been largely built upon the

word (specifically the word of the Christian Scriptures). We therefore tend to forget that people can communicate in other ways. Sometimes an intuitive awareness of the other's presence is sufficient to convey a message. This often happens when people are working closely and harmoniously together: there comes a point when it is no longer necessary to explain what has to be done next; it becomes intuitive. At times, such intuition can seem almost miraculous as, for example, when musicians who are very familiar with each other's style of playing seem able to anticipate what the other will do. Perhaps, when applied to our relationship with God, this is what Paul meant by having 'the mind of Christ' (1 Corinthians 2:16).

Another important form of non-verbal communication is our actions. For example, when we give someone a gift we are conveying a message. God also may communicate through actions. His unique relationship with creation means that both our circumstances and extraordinary events (or miracles) may be forms of divine communication.

The various ways in which we might hear God's voice will be described in greater detail in subsequent chapters.

The scope of God's guidance

In what areas of my life should I seek God's guidance? Are there certain aspects of life in which God takes a particular interest?

For example, Christians often seek God when

making *vocational or career choices*. Quite properly, they want to know in what sphere God is calling them to serve him. They take for granted a degree of freedom in career choice.

We tend to forget that this degree of vocational freedom is a recent development. It has emerged only in this century because of modern working practices combined with the erosion of the older social hierarchies. A couple of generations ago, freedom of choice with respect to career was much less prevalent. As a young man, Lawrence's father wanted to go to sea, but his father was an engineer and family pressure led him in that direction as well. If you were a woman, the opportunities at that time were even more restricted. For many women, marriage was the only way of escape from the prospect of a life spent caring for ageing parents. Those who did break into the world of work were likely to be restricted to unskilled shop or factory work, or to the lower echelons of some of the caring professions. If you did have some degree of choice in your career, that choice was probably irrevocable. You entered a profession or joined a company for life.

It is also the case that not everyone has benefited from this increased freedom of vocational choice. A bewildering array of possibilities may confront a university graduate. By contrast, an unskilled sixteen-year-old may face only the prospect of long-term unemployment.

For those who are fortunate enough to have a degree of freedom in this area, the ever-increasing complexity and flexibility of our culture can make the choice of career seem formidable. On the other hand, flexibility of working practices and the fluidity of the world of work mean that career choices are no longer irrevocable. It becomes possible to experiment with different careers. Changing jobs or employers no longer means a loss of seniority. One area where this is particularly noticeable is in Christian ministry: an increasing number of men and women are entering full-time Christian work after spending some years in secular employment.

Christians also often seek guidance when considering *marriage*. Like career choice, this is an area in which our freedom has increased significantly in recent times. It is also an area where the blueprint view of God's guidance has had a particularly pernicious effect. The combination of the belief that God has singled out for you a unique marriage partner, together with the Christian belief in the permanency of marriage, has serious implications. It means that, if you make a mistake in this area, you are condemning yourself and your partner to a life of God's second best. The illogicality of this view becomes apparent as you explore its further implications. Your marriage to Mr or Miss Wrong may mean that you have condemned a Miss or Mr Right to God's second best because you failed to marry her or him. If that person has married someone else, that marriage too must be God's second best and somewhere else yet another person, through no fault of their own, may have been condemned to God's second best, and so on indefinitely!

Instead of this static view of God's will, it makes

much more sense to see God's will as dynamic and flexible, and to see marital choice (as far as it exists for us) as an area of responsible freedom.

Vocational and marital choices are, of course, major personal decisions, and it is perfectly proper to seek God's guidance in these areas. However, it is easy to fall into the trap of assuming that God is only concerned with the big personal decisions. Recalling that God is a loving Father, it should be clear that he will be there for us in every decision that causes us anxiety, and in every decision that doesn't.

Since God is God of the whole of life, we should not try to limit him to the personal dimension. So, for example, our *political decisions* ought to come within the scope of God's guidance. It is striking that many books on guidance or Christian decision-making completely ignore this aspect of our lives. Yet it is precisely at this point that Christians have, in the past, made the greatest impact on the world in which they lived. Take, for example, the abolition of slavery: the political pressure for this change came from Christian laypeople in the face of considerable resistance from the political, economic and ecclesiastical establishment of their day.

Political freedom means far more than the right to put a cross on a ballot paper every few years. It is about our Christian responsibility to influence for good the society in which we live. This goes beyond campaigns for family values, or against abortion, or for keeping Sunday special. We need to make responsible decisions about the political and social issues of our day. What should concern me? How should I express that concern? Should I join a political party? Or would my concerns be more effectively expressed through a cross-party pressure group?

God guides on a 'need-to-know' basis

This final point is an important aspect of what we may expect when we listen for God's guidance. God does not communicate with us merely to satisfy our idle curiosity. Jesus made that very plain in his reply to Peter's question about John's future: 'If I want him to remain alive until I return, what is that to you? You must follow me' (John 21:22). God's communication with us is always so that we may follow Jesus more effectively. He empowers us for service.

God does not generally give us a bird's-eye view of what lies ahead. He does not need to, because he intends to be with us every step of the way. When the guide is with you, he does not need to explain what lies far ahead.

In a letter to his wife, Bishop Lesslie Newbigin recounts one of the early meetings of the World Council of Churches:

> Karl Barth gave us a tremendous oration on the funda-
> mental theme of the conference. It was real prophecy
> and compelled everyone, I think, to look beyond all our
> plans and self-importance to the living God. Some people
> were very annoyed by it, but I more and more feel that
> it was needed. In the evening at the reception Paul

Maury asked me what I thought of it. I said, 'It was magnificent, but where do we go from there?' Just at that moment Barth appeared, so Maury repeated my question to him. He said, 'Into the next room of course', and went! Which was the right answer; I mean that Barth demolishes all one's plans with his terrific prophetic words, and one is left wondering what to do next; and his answer always is, Just get on with the next plain duty.[5]

We do not need to formulate grand schemes or master plans. In fact, to do so may be to usurp God's authority. Knowing too much about what is to come gives us a false sense of independence. If God simply gave us the overall plan and let us get on with things, we could take pride in our own achievements, rather than giving him the thanks.

On the other hand, too much information about the future could paralyse us with fear. Some wit once remarked that if parents knew what they were doing when they had children they would be too terrified to go ahead! Whether this is true or not, most of us have benefited from experiences that we would have tried to avoid if we had known in advance what they would involve.

The final, liberating, prerequisite for a Christian approach to divine guidance is this realization that we do not need to know in detail what lies ahead. As Christians, we are assured of something far better than the script for the cosmic drama. God, the Great Playwright, is with us in every scene guiding us through our parts, enabling us to ad lib when the unexpected happens. This promise, that God is with us every step of the way, fosters trust and encourages communication with our divine guide.

Three

The Bible and guidance

> Your word is a lamp to my feet and a light
>   for my path.
>
> (Psalm 119:105)

This is just one of many similar assertions to be found within Scripture. Throughout the ages, God's people have reaffirmed that, in some sense, the words of Scripture function like light, enabling us to see more clearly on the pilgrimage of life.

We cannot simply read God's will for our lives directly from the pages of Scripture, however. Our circumstances are dramatically different from those of people in Bible times. We live in a complex and rapidly changing world. The range of issues on which we are called to make responsible decisions is quite different. Much as we might like it to, the Bible simply does not give straight answers to many of the pressing questions we are facing.

The questions we have to ask in this chapter are: In what sense is Scripture like a light? What role may we expect the Bible to play in guidance and Christian decision-making?

A revealing light

When we speak of the Bible as revelation, we mean far more than that it is a historical record of God's dealings with the Jewish people. Revelation, properly understood, is an act of self-disclosure. I may know a great deal about you and yet not know you at all. If I want to get to know you as a person, I have to wait for you to reveal yourself to me.

Through the activity of the Holy Spirit, Scripture does not merely reveal certain truths about God. Rather, it is the primary means through which God reveals himself. It is a meeting-place with God. Perhaps it is not the only meeting-place (God is sovereign and may choose to meet us in other ways), but the testimony of Christians throughout the centuries is that Scripture is a sure meeting-place. Canon Graham Kings has expressed this in a meditative poem based on John 1. He calls it 'The Gospel of the Song':

> In the beginning were the Words,
> And the words were the Poet's,
> And were part of Him:
> They were lively and brilliant.
>
> And the Words became music,
>   and were sung,
>   full of beauty and freedom.
>
> We have heard the Song,
>   and been utterly moved,
>   again and again.

We had read poetry before,
    but beauty and freedom
    came through this Song.

No one has ever seen the Poet:
    this one Song, which is in His heart,
    has shown Him to us.

Scripture is the primary means through which God communicates with us today, but the purpose of that communication is communion, not information. Nevertheless, while introducing us to God, Scripture does tell us a great deal about him. After all, ignorance of the other person is no part of a mature personal relationship.

Scripture tells us not only about who God is but also about his wishes for his creation. We often ask, 'What is God's will?' Yet God has already revealed much of his will in Scripture. Theologians often refer to this as 'God's moral will', because it includes the ethical teaching of both Old and New Testaments.

Much of God's will is already in the public domain. He has clearly shown what he expects of his human creatures concerning morality, worship, responsible stewardship, and so on. However, his revealed will takes the form of principles and norms rather than detailed blueprints.

That's all very well, you may say. But what have general standards of conduct to do with God's will for my life? What is the role of biblical principles in relation to personal guidance or decision-making?

As we have already suggested, such standards are vitally important as a precondition for guidance. If we are knowingly flouting God's revealed will, why should we expect him to guide in a more specific way? If we are being deliberately disobedient on some matter about which Scripture has spoken clearly, why should we expect our decision-making to reflect God's will?

Scripture provides us with standards by which we may judge all claims to be doing God's will. They mark out the boundaries within which our decisions must lie if we are to make any sense of the notion of 'Christian' decision-making. Bill Hybels, Senior Pastor of Willow Creek Community Church, makes the point graphically when he writes:

> Almost every month someone tells me he is being led to be unfaithful to his wife. He thinks he is being led to the woman God chose for him, and that his marriage is a regrettable mistake – a sin, even. The only way he can do God's will, he tells me, is to repent of his sin and unite his life with the woman he should have married in the first place.
>
> The rationalizations are often very sophisticated, but the bottom line is always the same: people want to divorce the spouses to whom they were joined in holy matrimony in order to marry others who seem more attractive. This is not a leading from God: I can say that unequivocally.[1]

The reason Bill Hybels can be so sure is that such behaviour contradicts the clear teaching of Scripture. We may choose to commit adultery. We may choose to lie, cheat or steal. And we may be certain that none of these is God's will because they are all explicitly forbidden in Scripture.

Of course, there will be hard cases. Sometimes, because of past sins (my own or those of other people), a choice of evils confronts me. I may be forced to choose the least evil option, but this does not transform it into a good. It remains an evil of which I must repent. In any case, though, such situations are rarer than our desire for self-justification would have us believe.

However, between these extremes, there are many situations where the Bible does not speak unequivocally. For example, most employment opportunities are not clearly immoral. The general principles laid down in Scripture will not help me to choose between accountancy and teaching.

It is worth noting that the Bible's function as a revealing light is by no means restricted to the level of personal morality. On the contrary, if we permit them to do so, biblical principles will help us see the society in which we live from a new perspective. This is the motivation behind much Christian social and political action. If we take the Bible seriously, we may find it challenging our allegiance to our culture in unexpected ways. This, too, is part of its guiding role: provoking the people of God to be salt and light in society.

Living in the light

Light is absolutely fundamental to normal human life. Without it, our capacity to work or to play, to avoid danger or to appreciate the beauties of God's creation, is severely limited. We might say the same of the light of God's Word.

We may try to use the light of Scripture in different ways, however. Some ways are better than others.

One popular but inappropriate way of using Scripture is to neglect it until we have a problem. Confronted with difficulties in our private or public life, we turn to the Bible to seek specific answers to specific questions. We might call this the flash-gun approach. Most of the time we are content to stumble about in the darkness. However, from time to time we stub our toes or our hand brushes against something that causes us to feel threatened. Then we turn on the light for a fraction of a second, just enough to help us deal with the immediate problem, before returning to the darkness.

Such a flash-gun approach to Scripture may take several different forms. Perhaps when we are in difficulties, we simply start reading in the hope that something will turn up to comfort us or shed light on our problems.

Alternatively, we may play Bible roulette. This is the tradition of asking a question and opening the Bible at random in the hope of finding an answer. We may play a similar 'game' with books of daily readings, Scripture calendars or promise boxes (small decorative boxes containing many compartments; in each compartment there is a piece of paper on which a biblical promise is printed).

Few writers on guidance commend such an approach, and yet it remains surprisingly popular. One of the most eloquent critiques of the practice comes from the pen of John Newton, the slave-trader who, after conversion, became a giant of evangelical spirituality. He wrote:

> Others, when in doubt, have opened the Bible at a venture, and expected to find something to direct them in the first verse they should cast their eye upon … Among the Romans the writings of Virgil were frequently consulted upon these occasions … And, indeed, Virgil is as well adapted to satisfy inquirers in this way, as the Bible itself; for if people will be governed by the occurrence of a single text of Scripture, without regarding the context or duly comparing it with the general tenor of the Word of God, and with their own circumstances, they may commit the greatest extravagances, expect the greatest impossibilities, and contradict the plainest dictates of common sense, while they think they have the Word of God on their side.[2]

There is a tendency to dismiss Bible roulette as the harmless aberration of immature Christians. But it is not at all harmless. On the contrary, it is a form of bibliomancy, a divinatory technique just like astrology. It constitutes a serious misuse of Scripture and betrays a lack of understanding of its purpose.

Of course, God may graciously adapt himself to our ignorance. So, for example, the apostles drew lots to choose a successor for Judas (Acts 1:26). Since they were not corrected, we may conclude that God used that method for making clear his will. On the other hand, as they grow in maturity, we hear no more about the drawing of lots.

Rather than being a flash-gun that we use at times

when we have exhausted our own resources, Scripture is intended to be a steady light. The psalmists discovered for themselves, and extolled in their poems of worship, the value of daily meditation on Scripture.

The purpose of Scripture is personal knowledge of God; communion rather than occasional encounter. Continuous exposure seems more appropriate therefore than rare flashes of light. In this it is not so very different from other forms of personal knowledge. Contrary to the myths of our instant success culture, friendship takes time; marriage takes time; parenthood takes time. All personal relationships take time. Even the basic skills we take for granted (such as reading, driving a car or using a keyboard) take time. The learner is immersed in them until they are so familiar that they become instinctive. The same is true of Scripture. The effect of continuous immersion is a gradual reshaping of our values and attitudes along more biblical lines: the transformation of our minds, spoken of in Romans 12:2.

A personal word from God?

If it is true that the Bible exists to enable and develop communion with God, we should expect more of it than merely a set of impersonal principles. We must always be open to the possibility that God will speak personally and specifically through the words of Scripture. However, this is not something we can force. As C. S. Lewis put it, 'Aslan is not a tame lion.' We cannot expect to manipulate our Creator into giving us advice in a particular way. This radical freedom on God's part serves to reinforce the inappropriateness of divinatory uses of Scripture (which are both impersonal and manipulative).

Dietrich Bonhoeffer used to read his Bible systematically with the help of daily readings published by the Moravian Brethren. Just before the outbreak of the Second World War he was in America. He was uneasy about this. He was homesick and longed to return to minister in Germany. His American friends were busy looking for ways to protect him by keeping him in America. Eventually, he decided to return but almost immediately felt guilty about letting his friends down. In this dark and uncertain situation, one of his daily readings included 2 Timothy 4:21, in which Paul asks Timothy to do his best to come to him before winter. Bonhoeffer wrote:

> That follows me around all day. It is as if we were soldiers home on leave, and going back into action regardless of what they were to expect. We cannot be released from it. Not as if we are essential, as if we were needed (by God?), but simply because that is where our life is, and because we abandon, destroy, our life if we are not back in the fight. It is not a matter of piety, but of something more vital. But the feelings through which God acts are not only the pious but also those vital ones. 'Do your best to come before winter' – it is not a misuse of Scripture if I apply that to myself. May God give me grace to do it.[3]

Another example comes from Edith Schaeffer's history of *L'Abri*. It was early 1955 and the Schaeffers were planning an open home where people could find spiritual nourishment and biblical truth. During her regular Bible reading, Edith was struck by the words of Isaiah 2:2:

> In the last days
> the mountain of the LORD's temple will be established
>   as chief among the mountains;
> it will be raised above the hills,
>   and all nations will stream to it.

She says:

> My feeling was one of excitement. I read it over again, and then again ... then reached for my pencil and wrote in the margin: 'Jan. '55, promise ... Yes, *L'Abri*'. For I had the tremendous surge of assurance that although this had another basic meaning, it was being used by God to tell me something. I did not feel that 'all nations' were literally going to come to our home for help, but I did feel that it spoke of people from many different nations coming to a house that *God* would establish for the purpose of making 'His ways' known to them ... It seemed to me that God was putting His hand on my shoulder in a very real way and that He was saying that there would be a work which would be His work, not ours, which man could not stop.[4]

A fortnight later the Schaeffers received notice that they were to be expelled from Switzerland! In the dark weeks that followed, that verse was a source of great reassurance. Had they not been convinced that God wanted them to stay in Switzerland, they might have taken their circumstances as a door closing and returned to America. Instead, a series of miraculous 'coincidences' led eventually to the expulsion order being rescinded.

As a rider to that story, note that Edith admits drawing various false conclusions from that verse. She assumed it was referring to the home they were then living in and began planning accordingly. In fact, the promise was fulfilled but not in the way she expected.

The personal words from God cited in these examples did not come as bolts from the blue. They were not the result of Bible roulette or another form of random dipping into Scripture. Rather, they emerged from a regular discipline of reading Scripture. In Bonhoeffer's case, the verse confirmed a course of action he had already decided upon but about which he was still uneasy. In Edith Schaeffer's case, it turned out to be a powerful reassurance in the face of an apparently insuperable difficulty.

If a verse or passage seems to strike me with the force of revelation, it is certainly right to take it seriously. God may be speaking through it.

However, there may be other explanations for such an experience. For example, a biblical injunction may touch a raw nerve, revealing that some aspect of my life is wrong and needs to be put right. If 'Thou shalt not steal' makes me feel guilty about all those pens, paper clips and envelopes that have made their way home from the office, God is speaking; but only in the general sense in which all of Scripture is God's Word.

Or I may latch on to a particular verse because it reinforces something I want to do already or because it seems to justify some hidden desire. This may be God speaking, or may simply be a way of justifying my desires to myself and others. There is a particularly poignant example of this from the life of the evangelist George Whitefield. His wife was expecting a child and, for some reason, Whitefield found certain biblical promises about John the Baptist particularly relevant. On the basis of these, he publicly declared that the child would be a son and a great prophetic figure. A son was duly born and named John. When he died four months later, Whitefield was honest enough to admit:

> I misapplied several texts of Scripture. Upon these grounds, I made no scruple of declaring 'that I should have a son, and that his name should be John'.[5]

Every word I apparently receive from God therefore needs to be carefully weighed. God may be speaking, but that does not relieve me of my responsibility to decide and to act. Specific words from Scripture may have a dramatic impact on my decision-making process but, under normal circumstances, they should not be allowed to short-circuit it. I must relate those words to my circumstances and my understanding of what would glorify God and serve his kingdom in this particular situation. Returning to the example of Paul cited earlier, he was faced with clear divine warnings of impending imprisonment. However, he did not change his mind about going to Jerusalem. He decided that his imprisonment would serve the gospel better at that point than would his freedom.

Four

Know yourself

Is the self relevant?

A couple of years ago, an acquaintance of ours moved to a new parish. As she settled in, she became aware that the parish was short of housegroup leaders. Since she was an experienced housegroup leader, she offered her services to the vicar and was refused. Instead, he wondered if she would be willing to fill a vacancy as the church's representative on the local council of churches. When our friend pointed out that she would not feel comfortable in that role, it was suggested that her gifts and feelings ought to take second place to God's will and the needs of the situation.

Another friend had a similar experience while looking for a parish in which to serve his curacy. One parish in particular seemed quite keen to have him. However, after prayer and reflection, he felt strongly that it was not the right place for him. The vicar was convinced otherwise, and wrote accusing him of putting his personal feelings before God's will.

It is easy to see how those vicars arrived at their point of view. Some biblical images of the Christian life seem to point in this direction. If Christians are slaves of God or soldiers in a spiritual conflict, then they are under orders. All that matters is discerning and obeying God's will. Their gifts, wishes and feelings are simply irrelevant.

Yet does this follow from the biblical image of Christians as servants of God or slaves to right-eousness (Romans 6:15–18)? As we have already seen, we are the servants of one who loves us and calls us his friends. To such a one, our gifts, wishes and feelings will not be irrelevant. On the contrary, they are an integral part of who God created us to be. We can trust God to guide in ways that take full account of who we are. This is well illustrated by the example of Daniel: his natural gifts (Daniel 1:4) and his subsequent training in the language and culture of a pagan court were crucial to what God called him to do. Similarly Paul, with his zealous personality, his upbringing in a Hellenistic environment and his rabbinic training, was shaped by his gifts and his circumstances to be the ideal apostle to the Gentiles.

Of course, God may overrule our wishes from time to time. Dr Ken McAll gives the following example:

> As I was driving home from work, I was held up at a traffic light. As my frustration and impatience grew I felt the Lord was directing me to turn left. I argued, 'No, I want to go straight home.' 'Turn left,' he commanded. I was alone so ... I turned left, feeling rather foolish. I

nevertheless drove very slowly so as not to miss anything. Then from the right-hand side of the road a woman's voice shouted, 'Doctor Ken! Doctor Ken!'[1]

The woman turned out to be a friend whom Dr McAll had not seen for eight years. What is more, she had been trying unsuccessfully to contact him all day because she had just heard that her brother was dying.

God is our Lord and sometimes he simply commands, as in this case. However, most of the time, he expects his servants to make responsible use of the gifts he has given them.

Personality and decision-making

Our personalities play an important role in shaping our whole approach to decision-making. One popular indicator of personality, the *Myers Briggs Type Indicator*, highlights a number of personality factors which are organized into four scales.[2]

Extroversion–Introversion (E/I) measures our preference for one of two complementary attitudes to the world. The extrovert prefers to focus on the external world of objects and people, while the introvert prefers the inner world of ideas and feelings. For the introvert, decision-making will be primarily a private internal process. By contrast, extroverts are likely to be more open to the social dimension of decision-making, actively seeking the advice of others and taking that into account.

Sensing–Intuition (S/N) measures our preferred way of perceiving this world: either by direct use of the five senses, or indirectly, by processing sensory information through the unconscious to produce intuitive responses. Our preference on this scale will affect the ways in which we gather the information on which our decisions will be based as well as the types of information that strike us as significant. 'Sensing' individuals tend to focus on concrete realities. They are particularly sensitive to the facts and figures, to the practical details which are so important in deciding whether a particular course of action is feasible. Intuitive people, on the other hand, tend to be more possibility-oriented, and may overlook the practical details in order to pursue a particularly interesting course of action.

Thinking–Feeling (T/F) is the scale that most directly concerns our decision-making. It indicates our preference for either of two complementary ways of making decisions: one based on impersonal logical criteria, the other on more subjective criteria. The term 'feeling' in this context is rather misleading, since it refers to ethical and aesthetic factors as well as personal and social ones. A 'thinking' person, in this sense of the term, is likely to adopt a detached, objective attitude to the decision-making process. Conversely, a 'feeling' person will approach a decision in a more subjective way, perhaps more conscious of the personal and social ramifications of the decision.

Finally, *Judging–Perceiving* (J/P) indicates whether we relate to the world around us primarily by means of our judging (T/F) or our perceiving functions (S/N). Again, our preference on this scale will have a significant impact on our decision-making. 'Judging' individuals approach life with their preferred decision-making function (thinking or feeling) to the fore. They therefore appear more decisive and organized than their 'perceiving' fellows. They like everything to be under control and may become impatient with life's inevitable loose ends. At times, they may even become impatient with God. By contrast, 'perceiving' people are slower to make decisions. They are more tolerant of what is happening around them and to them. They are more likely to go with the flow, to 'let go and let God'.

Together, these and other factors not covered by the Indicator interact to create the rich diversity of human personalities. Inevitably they colour the way in which we make decisions. Part of the self-knowledge which is helpful for making responsible decisions, therefore, will be an awareness of how our particular personality is likely to bias our decisions. One of the reasons why the advice of others is so important in decision-making is precisely because different personalities are able to throw fresh light upon the situation, and so free us to some extent from the effect of our own personal bias.

Discerning our gifts

Every human being is unique. Each individual has a unique genetic inheritance and is influenced by different familial, social and cultural constraints. To complicate matters still further, everyone is free to respond to those influences in different ways. The result is a unique mixture of personality, aptitude and preferences.

To the secular mind, these are just brute facts. They are givens: the biological and social constraints within which the human being operates. One may accept them or revolt against them, but they are nothing more than accidents.

Christianity adds a rich new dimension to this aspect of human existence. It points out that these factors are not just brute facts. On the contrary, they are the gifts of a caring creator God.

When you look at human aptitudes in this way, it is natural to apply the teaching of the parable of the talents to them. These gifts are given not merely for self-fulfilment but for the common good and the building up of God's kingdom. As John White points out,

> If God has imparted natural abilities to us, we should think very seriously before deciding not to develop and use them.[3]

However, this cannot be reduced to a simple formula: 'I am very good at mathematics. Therefore, God must want me to be a mathematician.'

To begin with, most gifts may be used in a variety of ways. God may want me to become an accountant rather than a mathematician. Furthermore, a particular aptitude does not necessarily mean that I am called to make a career of it. God may want me to pursue another vocation entirely, while offering my ability with numbers to the local church by becoming its treasurer.

Another complication is that most of us have more gifts than we could possibly develop. Human beings are among the least specialized of God's creatures:

much of our success as a species is due to our ability to adapt to different situations. If I choose to develop one of my gifts, I am, by implication, choosing not to develop others. Einstein might have become a concert violinist (or so several of his acquaintances have claimed). However, he chose to develop his mathematical skills instead.

A century before Einstein, there was another very gifted young mathematician. His name was Henry Martyn, and he was assured of a glittering academic career in Cambridge. Instead, he chose to develop his aptitude for languages and dedicate that to the service of God. He became a missionary and translated the New Testament into three languages before dying at the age of thirty-one.

More recently there is the example of Dr Martyn Lloyd-Jones. As a young doctor he showed great potential and became assistant to the Royal Physician, Lord Horder. However, he also had an outstanding gift as an expository preacher. Finding that he could not do justice to both, he chose to develop the latter.

The point is that our natural gifts are not obligations but God-given possibilities. Just because I have, say, a gift for making music, it does not oblige me to seek a career in music. Rather, it places upon me the responsibility to consider what use, if any, I will make of that gift.

But how am I to choose between the gifts that God has given me? Is there some kind of hierarchy? Are there biblical criteria for such a choice? Are some more spiritual than others? If so, does God expect me to choose the latter instead of the former?

It is sometimes suggested that 'more spiritual' gifts, such as preaching, automatically take priority over 'lesser' gifts. But this is an unbiblical distinction. In 1 Corinthians 12, Paul makes it clear that *all* gifts are given by God for the good of the community. None is more spiritual than any other. Luther makes the following comment on this point:

> If you ask an insignificant maidservant why she scours a dish or milks the cow she can say: I know that the thing I do pleases God, for I have God's word and command-ment ... God does not look at the insignificance of the acts but at the heart that serves Him in such little things.[4]

It follows that, if there is a criterion, it is not that some gifts are more spiritual than others. The criterion lies in Paul's stipulation 'for the common good' (1 Corin-thians 12:7). But, again, this is not a simple formula for quick and easy career decisions.

Making an informed choice between your gifts assumes that you have some idea of what your gifts are to begin with. Unfortunately, for many people this is not so because of the circumstances which have shaped their lives. The expectations of parents, teach-ers and society have channelled them in a particular direction, and they are unaware, or only vaguely aware, of other possibilities.

Some gifts only emerge as a result of prior training. A novelist must first be able to write! Musicians and artists must learn to use the tools of their trade. A child with a natural aptitude for music may never discover it because an unmusical family has denied him or her the opportunity.

This is true also of abilities such as preaching and evangelism. Some people seem to have a natural ability to speak about Jesus in public or get alongside others and share the gospel. But important aspects of preaching and evangelism can be taught, and there are many more people who have latent gifts in these areas just waiting for appropriate training.

How then do we build up a fuller picture of where our gifts and abilities actually lie? In the case of natural gifts, school reports and the advice of mature friends are obviously very important. But these may be blinkered by the values of the school or the friend.

A more objective approach might be to try some of the many aptitude tests that are now available. These may highlight abilities that family, friends and school have overlooked. For example, Lawrence discovered in this way that he was potentially quite adept at learning languages. This came as something of a surprise since he had found school French very dull. However, these tests will not reveal all. They have mostly been designed with modern business needs in mind and therefore highlight those abilities which are of most use in the marketplace. In fact, having filled in a particularly complex computerized aptitude test as an undergraduate, Lawrence was informed that he ought to seek a job as a statistician with the Civil Service!

What about spiritual gifts? Here the recognition of the community is very important indeed. God has given the whole range of gifts for building up the body of Christ. Therefore Christian leaders should always be on the look-out for people who appear to be exercising a spiritual gift. When Diana was a teacher, she belonged to a church that took this responsibility seriously. They did not simply assume that because she was a teacher, the church should use her in this way. Instead, they discerned a latent gift for pastoral care, and they nurtured that gift by means of appropriate training and a support group. Because of that discernment, she is now an Anglican priest rather than a schoolteacher.

Dissatisfaction and desires

Many people are dissatisfied with their lives. They have some idea (perhaps very vague or even distorted) of what the ideal life would look like. In our culture, this ideal is fed by glamorous or romantic media images of the lifestyles of the rich and famous. For most people the reality falls far short of the ideal. The result is the common human experience of dissatisfaction, with its attendant dreams and desires.

Christian experience is very similar. We are only too aware of the present reality: we are fallen creatures in a twisted world. At the same time, we have experienced a call from God; a call to personal, social and cosmic perfection. The gap between this ideal and this reality results in a tension so great that at times it feels almost unbearable. Witness Paul's outburst, 'What a wretched man I am! Who will rescue me from this body of death?' (Romans 7:24). In Christian experience that tension leads to visions of the kingdom.

Everyone has dreams, desires and visions. But, for most people, they remain fragmentary and elusive.

They are not sufficiently clear to be a spur to action.

One reason for this lack of clarity is the sheer busyness of the culture in which we live. The pressures imposed by modern working practices upon those who have a job mean that they are simply too busy to pay attention to their dreams and desires. And when they get home from work, they are too exhausted for such things.

Perhaps more serious is the passivity (even apathy) engendered by the entertainment industry. It offers tired men and women instant, vicarious wish fulfilment. For a few precious hours each day they can escape from the uncomfortable realities of life. The danger is that the fantasy becomes a substitute for attempts to do something about the reality.

Because of this busyness and passivity, many people are unable to pay attention to the gap between reality and their ideals. They continually hurry along with a vague sense of unease that they cannot pin down.

How do we break out of this treadmill and begin to build our fragmentary desires into a coherent vision, with the potential to change not only our lives but perhaps also many others?

We must take time to attend to our dreams. One way to do this is to schedule regular quiet days and retreats into our calendar.[5] This should be a priority whenever we get a new diary: the creation of inviolable spaces that enable us to put the rest of life in perspective.

In those times we should listen to our anger and discontent. It is a mistake to assume that such feelings are necessarily sinful. We need to recognize honestly that all is not well. By owning and examining such feelings, we may begin to identify points where change is needed.

However, we must also look for signs of hope. Condemning an individual, organization or institution out of hand is only too easy. It is more satisfying for everything to be black and white but it is also usually dishonest. Most situations have their good points. We need to pay attention to these alongside the bad points.

Having honestly assessed the situation, we may ask how it would look if God's will for that situation was realized. Given this vicar or that boss; this set of expectations or that cluster of limitations, how might one begin to express the reality of God's reign right now? What would it mean to live a life of peace (in the biblical sense of wholeness) in this community?

As we take time to pay attention to them, we will find that our fragmentary desires begin to take on a more coherent shape. We will begin to see connect-ions between formerly unrelated fragments. Themes will begin to appear.

However, there are two points to bear in mind in relation to our dreams and visions. First, we may have visions of the possible shape of God's kingdom in our situations. But we should not take this to mean that we are somehow capable of bringing about the kingdom by our own efforts. On the other hand, the fact that the kingdom is God's, and can only come about at his instigation, does not mean that we can stand idly by. God has called us to be participants in his building of the kingdom. Our dreams and visions may be tiny elements in his cosmic plan.

A vision of this kind is therefore not in itself a call to action. Rather, it is another dimension to be brought into the process of discerning God's will.

Listening to the still, small voices

Some Christians give the impression that the whole decision-making process is a neat package: an essentially straightforward exercise in the use of sanctified common sense. God renews our minds, and we use our renewed minds to make sensible decisions.

Unfortunately, reality is not that tidy. By introducing the dimension of visions of what might be, we have already hinted that there is more to the human psyche than our common sense or our conscious reasoning powers. That 'more' plays a very important part in traditional understandings of divine guidance.

We may picture the conscious mind as a fertile plain ringed by high mountains. The ego, the centre of consciousness, is a castle at the centre of the plain. From our vantage-point in the castle, we can make a good job of mapping the plain.

But what lies beyond the mountains? Since the Enlightenment, western culture has argued that there is nothing beyond the mountains. It has ignored or ridiculed any evidence to the contrary. However, the persistence of 'visitors' from beyond the mountains (irrational urges, unexplained feelings, images, voices, *etc.*) strongly suggests that something is there.

In the twentieth century people are again taking these visitors seriously. Some of them can be identified as exiles returning (*e.g.* painful memories that have been suppressed). His success in identifying some of these exiles led Sigmund Freud to argue that all such visitors are exiles in disguise. By contrast, his one-time disciple, Carl Jung, argued that recurring themes among these visitors pointed to their common origin beyond the mountains. So he used them to begin mapping the unconscious dimension of the psyche.

Dreams and guidance

Among the most familiar visitors from beyond the mountains are dreams. The Bible is full of examples of significant dreams: dreams through which God spoke to people. Often the word was a word of warning or advice. For example, the Magi were warned not to return to Herod (Matthew 2:12) and Joseph is warned to flee to Egypt (Matthew 2:13) by means of dreams. Similarly, dreams played a part in Christian experience until the impact of the Enlightenment. Today, largely because of a renewed interest in dreams in the wider culture, Christians are again taking them more seriously.[6]

Dreams can play a role in guidance. Of course, for them to function in this way, I must take them seriously. As I pay attention to my dreams and become familiar with their themes and symbols, I may begin to recognize symbolic references to everyday life. Dreams are often coded reminders of things we have forgotten to do or are anxious about. As an extension of this, they may serve as warnings, *e.g.* a dream about a car crash may be a warning about my behaviour on the road or my neglect of the car. Yet other dreams may be predictive in character. A well-known example is Jung's dream of Europe awash with blood shortly before the outbreak of the First World War.

Sometimes dreams can be explained only in terms of divine communication. A striking example is a dream which affected a friend's choice of parish. He and his wife were looking for a parish close to a family member who was terminally ill. However, he had been sponsored by a diocese in another part of the country. When that bishop suggested a possible post, they reluctantly agreed to look at it.

Shortly before their visit, the wife had a vivid dream about the parish. In it she saw lakes and pine woods. Also in the dream was a sermon beginning with the words, 'This is none other than the house of the Lord.' Since the parish was in a large industrial city, they did not take the dream too seriously.

During the interview, they attended a service in the parish. Imagine their surprise when, after pinning up a picture of a large building, the outgoing curate began his sermon with the words, 'No, it isn't the town hall. This is none other than the house of the Lord'! Afterwards they had some spare time so they decided to drive round the parish. Again, imagine their surprise when the streets of terraced houses gave way to a series of man-made lakes set in pine woods!

Notice that the dream did not tell them what to do. Rather, it forced them to look more carefully at a situation which, otherwise, they might have been inclined to refuse. Since the husband was already feeling more positive about the parish as a result of the interview, they interpreted this remarkable confirmation of the dream as indication that this was where they should be. Subsequently, their misgivings about leaving their dying relative were allayed when the person made a remarkable recovery.

The still, small voice

The still, small voice heard by Elijah (1 Kings 19:12) has become the foundation stone for a great deal of Christian teaching about listening to God. Yet what does it mean? Is it 'a still small voice' (AV) 'a low murmuring sound' (NEB), 'the soft whisper of a voice' (GNB), 'a gentle whisper' (NIV), or 'the sound of a gentle breeze' (JB)? The Hebrew (meaning literally 'voice of thin silence') can be interpreted in a variety of ways.

Was it literally a voice out of thin air? Was it an inner voice? Or was it something less articulate: Elijah's interpretation of an inner urge, leading or conviction?

Perhaps the point to draw from this is that God can speak in any of these ways. Scripture clearly attests to a God who speaks. And, since Augustine, western Christianity has consistently understood the depths of the soul to be our primary meeting-place with God. Gordon MacDonald describes this inner spiritual centre as a garden:

> This garden is a place where the Spirit of God comes to make self-disclosure, to share wisdom, to give affirmation or rebuke, to provide encouragement, and to give direction and guidance. When this garden is in proper order, it is a quiet place, and there is an absence of busyness, of defiling noise, of confusion.[7]

John White puts it almost poetically when he says:

Deep within your vast interior spaces (and inner space and outer space are all one in eternity) is a tabernacle God built to commune with you. From it he calls with tender urgency. And from the furthest reaches of your inner space an ache of yearning echoes back his call.[8]

The still, small voice: not just the voice of conscience, but God's own voice whispering in the very depths of your own psyche.

The quotation from Ken McAll earlier in this chapter is a very clear example of God speaking. A friend of ours had a similar striking experience as an undergraduate in Oxford. She needed a car for her church activities but had very little money and no idea how to find a decent vehicle. She describes how, one evening as she was studying, she 'felt that an inward voice … was saying, "Get up, and go out, and get on your bike."' At first, she ignored it, arguing that she was just imagining an excuse not to study. However, the pressure increased, until, feeling rather foolish, she did as she was told. For the next quarter of an hour she was directed around the streets of Oxford. Then the inner voice simply stopped. She got off her bike and looked around but could see no reason why she should have been brought here. Disappointed (and a little worried that she might be 'freaking out' because of overwork) she returned to her bike. It was then that she noticed a sign on the car next to her bike. It was for sale and it was within her very limited means. After getting a mechanically minded friend to confirm that it was roadworthy, she bought it.

Sometimes the inner voice may shed light on a major life-decision. As a sixth-former, another friend of ours was torn between joining the RAF and training for the Anglican ministry. He had more or less decided to do the former but his attraction to the priesthood refused to go away. One day, he was sitting chatting with schoolfriends when an entirely new thought came to him: 'Why not become an RAF chaplain?' As far as he can recall, no-one had ever mentioned this as a possibility. From that day on, he was convinced that this was the right way forward. That conviction has been confirmed by the fact that he has spent virtually his entire ministry as an RAF chaplain. To this day, he remains convinced that the idea was not his but was divinely inspired.

Sometimes that inner voice is less articulate – more of a pressure than a voice. A missionary friend of ours describes how a local woman was guided to help her at the hospital:

> Otilia had a growing desire to visit children in hospital … She'd thought of asking if she could join me on my visits but instead just prayed about it until one Wednesday in June she decided it was time for action. She prayed very specifically that God would guide her and, together with a friend, caught a bus to the Children's Hospital.
>
> There are probably some fifty wards in the hospital so on arrival her friend asked: 'Where are we going to go?'
>
> 'Let's go along here.' So they found their way to one of the old blocks, not the main building.
>
> 'Which floor?'

'How about the third floor?'

'Which ward?'

'Let's try this one,' said Otilia, as enthusiastic as ever.

That afternoon I too was in the hospital busily trying to help the children cut out and stick their models. It was particularly difficult as I was on my own and there seemed to be a lot of children with drips who needed extra help. As I turned round I suddenly found myself face to face with Otilia!

'What are you doing here?' I asked in astonishment. 'Is there a child here from Huascar?'

'No,' she replied. 'I just wanted to visit some children in hospital and God guided me here.'

Recently our friend has returned to this country, and Otilia now runs the hospital visiting scheme.

The importance of testing the spirits

However, dreams of the night and inner voices are not necessarily the messengers of God. In this century we know only too well the horrors perpetrated by those who claimed to be obeying such inner leadings. Small wonder that many people are suspicious of such things. The Bible as ever finds the right balance between credulity and scepticism. In his first letter, John advises us: 'Dear friends, do not believe every spirit, but test the spirits to see whether they are from God' (1 John 4:1).

Dreams and inner voices may reflect our own needs, either physical or psychological. Many warning and reminder dreams may be interpreted as the unconscious dimension of our psyche drawing our conscious attention to situations with which we need to deal. Other dreams may reflect our unconscious perceptions of the world around us. Our senses bombard us with far more information than we can ever consciously process. Much of this sinks straight into the unconscious where it is processed and may re-emerge as an intuition or urge. This is the rationale behind subliminal advertising, and it may also explain some predictive dreams.

Traditional Christian theology offers yet another set of possible sources for such dreams and inner voices. It speaks of a created spiritual realm parallel with the material creation. A good deal of the speculation about the unconscious since Jung's time suggests a large degree of overlap between these concepts. One might say that the unconscious is open to the realm of spiritual creation. If this is the case, then it raises the possibility of angelic or demonic influence.

The point of all this is to warn against assuming that dreams or inner voices that seem to convey messages or commands should be obeyed unthinkingly. Rather, we must test the spirits. We must treat dreams, voices, leadings and urges as further data for the process of responsible decision-making.

The heart's desire

James advises:

> Come near to God and he will come near to you. Wash your hands, you sinners, and purify your hearts, you double-minded (James 4:8).

From this, the Danish philosopher Søren Kierkegaard derived his famous epigram, 'Purity of heart is to will one thing.' This advice is often cited in relation to divine guidance and Christian discernment. But what does it mean?

Some people think that sheer force of will can overcome double-mindedness; that you should force yourself to concentrate on one thing to the exclusion of all else. But this can lead to an unhealthy obsessive attitude (*cf.* the modern phenomenon of work-aholism). One wonders whether such a state really deserves the description 'purity'!

Another way of interpreting James 4:8 is to say that such single-mindedness comes from identifying one's heart's true desire and aligning oneself accordingly. This may sound like a recipe for doing your own thing, but it makes a great deal of sense when taken together with one of the most profound things ever written by St Augustine. Addressing God, he says, 'You made us for yourself and our hearts find no peace until they rest in you.' God is the heart's true desire. Aligning one's own will with God's issues in peace.

The idea that conformity to God's will brings true peace has led to an important tradition of 'seeking the peace' as an indicator of divine guidance. If I am at peace about a particular course of action, it is suggested, that must be the will of God. The missionary Helen Roseveare recalls being advised as a student, 'Let the peace of God umpire in your heart; if He is speaking He will give peace and silence other voices.'[9]

An aid worker, describing his call to work with Cambodian refugees, has used the related idea of resonance. As he listened to a radio programme telling of the plight of the refugees, he felt as if he were a guitar string being made to resonate by a note of precisely the right pitch. He knew quite unequivocally that this was the right place for him to be, because his desire to serve was exactly in tune with their needs. That radio programme revealed to him his heart's desire.

Of course, you cannot take peace or the lack of it as an infallible guide to God's will. Lack of peace may be the result of a physical disorder, or of guilt brought about by bad teaching. On the other hand, someone may feel at peace about indulging in an extramarital affair or fiddling their tax return.

A balanced assessment of our feelings is offered by the Roman Catholic tradition of discernment that was begun by Ignatius of Loyola. He was forced to spend many weeks convalescing after receiving a leg injury during the Siege of Pamplona. To while away his time, he would fantasize about the world of chivalry. He also devoured the only books available to him: a Life of Christ and a book of the Lives of the Saints. Gradually he came to notice that the two pastimes affected him very differently. In his own words:

> When he was thinking of the things of the world he was filled with delight, but when afterwards he dismissed them from weariness, he was dry and dissatisfied. And when he thought of going barefoot to Jerusalem and of eating nothing but herbs and performing the other rigors he saw that the saints had performed, he was consoled, not only when he entertained these thoughts, but even

after dismissing them he remained cheerful and satisfied.[10]

The Ignatian tradition does not 'seek the peace' as a hallmark of God's will. Rather, it recognizes two clusters of feelings, consolation and desolation, which attend all our activities. By paying attention to these, it offers us a way of taking our feelings into account in the decision-making process. It treats them not as a final arbiter but as a dimension of the information upon which we base the decision.

Consolation includes a sense of being at peace with God, the world and ourselves. It may also be experienced as confidence in God, gratitude for all that God has given me, or a desire for the greater good or for the opportunity for sacrificial service. Sometimes it may superficially seem uncomfortable, *e.g.* an awareness of my own sinfulness and my need for God's forgiveness. In short, feelings of consolation are all those feelings, positive or negative, that drive me towards God.

Conversely, feelings of desolation drive me away from God. They include self-hatred, a sense that one's life is empty and meaningless, loss of confidence in God and God's love, and desires that take us away from God.

Awareness of my sinfulness may be an experience of either consolation or desolation. My assessment of it will depend upon its effects. If it traps me in a vicious circle of remorse and guilt, it is an example of desolation. If it enables me to receive God's forgiveness, it is an example of consolation.

The point is that we should not be guided by these feelings, but rather pay attention to them and consider what they might have to say about the courses of action with which they are associated. For example, if I have difficulty praying when contemplating a particular course of action, that action bears closer and more critical examination. It is all part of the process of gathering adequate information on which to base a major life-decision.

Self-knowledge is a prerequisite for Christian discernment. Looking realistically at my feelings about a particular decision (and, particularly, its impact on my relationship with God) is an important defence against self-delusion.

Five

Circumstantial evidence

The importance of limits

In the last chapter we explored the importance of self-knowledge in relation to guidance. An important element of such knowledge is a realistic assessment of my gifts (both natural and spiritual). However, I do not exercise those gifts in a vacuum. Equally important are the circumstances within which I have to operate.

It is not always easy to distinguish between circumstances and gifts. Most people would be inclined to place outstanding artistic or sporting abilities in the latter category. Similarly, they would classify a serious physical disability as an unfortunate circumstance.

Perhaps the simplest rule of thumb is as follows. If it creates possibilities for me, it is a gift. If it places limits upon me, it is a circumstance (as the etymology of the word suggests, it is that which stands around me, which hems me in).

There is, however, a grey area between the two. The pianist Paul Wittgenstein lost his right arm in the

First World War, but that did not destroy his career. On the contrary, his disability became the catalyst for several original compositions.

At the age of seven, Glenn Cunningham's legs were seriously burned. The doctors decided against amputation, but told his parents that he would never walk again. When they told the boy, he replied, 'I want to walk and run, and I will.' Because of his determination, Glenn was running (even if slowly) two years later. Eventually he went to college. He was still running, but now he was running because he enjoyed it and was good at it. At the Berlin Olympics he broke the Olympic record in the 1500-metre race. The following year, he broke the world record for the indoor mile. An unfortunate circumstance was the catalyst that unleashed a world-beating talent.

Many people regard freedom as absence of constraints. Yet this is highly misleading because, taken literally, it turns freedom into an unrealistic ideal. We are finite creatures, and are limited in all kinds of obvious (and not so obvious) ways by our very finitude.

What is more, those limits enable us to be genuinely free. Even the libertarian philosopher, Edmund Burke, could write 'Liberty ... must be limited to be possessed.' Unlimited freedom of action is not so much liberating as terrifying.

Anyone who has lived or worked with young children knows that they need clearly defined limits. A child presented with two or three options for breakfast has genuine freedom of choice. The same child faced with ten or twenty options is merely bewildered. Even as adults, we sometimes find that the sheer variety of choices available in our culture is bewildering.

To shield ourselves from such unwelcome freedom we create protective boundaries. Indeed, much of human culture is precisely about such boundaries: taboos, mores, class distinctions, customs, laws. It would not be a great exaggeration to understand society as a network of protective boundaries against the terrifying possibilities of the world we inhabit.

The need for limits is particularly clear in artistic activity. If you give a child a box of oil paints or a keyboard and ask that child to let his or her imagination run riot, what is the result? Unless the child is exceptional, you can expect a noise or a mess. Genuine creativity requires imagination plus discipline. An artist must learn the limits as well as the possibilities of his or her medium.

In relation to important life-decisions, circumstances play a similar role to that of the limits imposed upon the artist by their chosen medium. Some circumstances that shape my decision-making are the result of my unique genetic inheritance and upbringing. Then there are the chances and mischances that I have encountered so far.

Beyond this ring of purely personal limitations are the limits created by the culture in which I live and its relation to other cultures. A throwaway remark made by Jacob Bronowski during his television series *The Ascent of Man* epitomizes the power of these limits. Referring to the mathematician John von Neumann, he comments:

He was born in 1903, the son of a Jewish family in Hungary. If he had been born a hundred years earlier, we would never have heard of him. He would have been doing what his father and grandfather did, making rabbinical comments on dogma.[1]

Where, when and to whom I am born can dramatically affect my life story. For most of the human race and for most of human history, circumstances have been far more powerful than the individual's ability to exercise freedom. Being born into the wrong race could consign one to slavery or the obscurity of the ghetto. Being born a woman rather than a man would almost certainly result in less scope for personal freedom. Conversely, being born into the ruling élite of a culture usually means much greater freedom than being born into its lower echelons.

What has this to do with guidance or Christian decision-making? My circumstances are important precisely because they are the context in which God calls me. If the Christian life may be likened to a work of art, my personal and cultural circumstances are the characteristics of the medium with which God wants me to work.

This does not mean that I am entirely bound by my circumstances. On the contrary, they become the means through which I can express my love for God. The sonnet is a demanding poetic form that severely limits the poet's freedom. Nevertheless, Shakespeare and many other poets have shown repeatedly that being creative even within such limits is quite possible. The form is the occasion for the creativity.

I might say the same of my circumstances. They limit me, but they also make my living of the Christian life real. In a sense they become gifts rather than limitations. This may sometimes be hard to acknowledge and, often, only the person who is experiencing those circumstances has the right to acknowledge them as God's gift. So only Joni Eareckson herself could say of the wheelchair in which she is confined, 'I'm beginning to see the chair more as a tool than a tragedy.'[2]

Christian decision-making involves a realistic assessment of our circumstances. Together, they make up the situation in which God has placed us. The question should be how can we best serve him in these circumstances.

Complexity and constraints

We live in a culture which offers us great freedoms. Yet we also live in a very complex culture, and its very complexity imposes upon us new kinds of constraint.

Perhaps the most commonplace example of the complexity of our culture is the dazzling array of goods for sale in every shop and supermarket. Our society highly values consumer choice. But why is this? Why should we want to have to choose between thirty brands of washing-powder whenever we visit the supermarket? In a helpful analysis of contemporary views of freedom, the theologian Richard Bauckham points out that consumer choice has been identified with a basic value of our culture: freedom of opportunity. He argues:

> Freedom of opportunity in fact comes down, more than anything else, to consumer choice, the freedom to take advantage of endlessly increasing opportunities to spend money … The freedom we are all encouraged to want is the freedom to have more and more of what can be bought, to enjoy more and more of what can be bought.[3]

The poet Baudelaire once pointed out that novelty was the distinguishing characteristic of modern culture. Consumer choice gives people access to that novelty. Provided they have the spending power, they can always buy a new experience, and that capacity to buy new experiences creates the illusion of freedom. Beneath this apparent freedom, however, lurk a number of hidden constraints.

One of those constraints is an addiction to novelty. Fashion dominates over utility. It is no longer just clothes that are discarded year by year as new fashions appear. For example, businesses now change their computer systems with monotonous regularity. This is not because the change makes them more efficient, but because it conveys the right image. All too often, churches latch on to the latest fashion in evangelism or spiritual experience for much the same reason. We are addicted to change for change's sake, perhaps because we naïvely assume that change is evidence of growth and progress.

In a culture besotted by consumerism, poverty is a very clear constraint. It prevents its victims from being full members of that society. However, prosperity brings its own constraints. There is a tremendous social pressure to conform to the consumption patterns of your peers. So, while money may bring freedom of choice, it also makes it harder to choose not to choose! This is seen most clearly in children and young people: the teenager who simply can't go to school without the right brand of designer trainers; the little boy who simply must have the latest computer game; the irresistible choices for character toys from the latest film or TV series. However, it also affects adults. Many of our friends are surprised to discover that we do not have an automatic dishwasher.

Some time ago we realized that our increasingly busy lifestyle as full-time Christian workers was gradually destroying our family life. After much agonizing, we concluded that we had to cut back on our work commitments. Apparently, this is not the 'right answer' in contemporary middle-class England. A local clergyman was shocked by our decision. He told us we should hire an *au pair* to look after the children and free us more effectively for Christian ministry!

Paradoxically, increased freedom of choice may result in a paralysis of our capacity for rational decision-making. A Greek fable tells of a donkey who starved to death between a pile of hay and a pile of carrots: he was unable to choose between them. The increasing complexity of our culture may be taking us in that direction. How do you choose between a hundred makes of computer? There just isn't time to examine each option and make an informed choice. Instead, people may make an arbitrary choice, or take refuge in a familiar brand name, or limit themselves to a single criterion ('It was the cheapest one available'), or rely upon expert advice (the salesman, a *Which?* report, a review in the relevant journal).

The information explosion and rapid changes in our social structures are doing for political and social choices what the hypermarket has done for consumer choice. We are faced with so much information and such complex and rapidly changing situations that we may shrink from the challenge of responsible decision-making. Either we refuse to decide, leaving the decisions to experts or leaders. Or we choose by criteria that are entirely irrational.

Doors: open or closed?

One way in which Christians sometimes seek to reduce the complexity of the options open to them is by asking God to open or close doors. You will frequently hear it said that God indicates his will regarding a particular course of action either by smoothing out the way for it or by blocking it. Suppose someone feels called to the Christian ministry. If the relevant selection boards do not support this sense of calling, he or she might conclude that God was 'closing the door' on this plan. Conversely, if a clear opportunity for Christian service becomes apparent to that person, he or she may seize upon it as God 'opening a door'.

Those who believe in this means of guidance cite a variety of New Testament precedents in its favour. Paul occasionally speaks of doors being opened for ministry, *e.g.* 'I went to Troas ... and found that the

Lord had opened a door for me' (2 Corinthians 2:12). Similarly, John reports the following message to the church in Philadelphia: 'I have placed before you an open door that no-one can shut' (Revelation 3:8).

Traditional books on guidance sometimes give the impression that the opening or closing of doors is a clear indication of God's will. If God opens a door, we ought to have the faith to go through it. Conversely, if God closes a door, we should be obedient and accept his decision as final.

However, matters are not as straightforward as this might suggest. These are not literal doors whose degree of openness can be measured with physical measuring instruments. To say that a door has opened or closed on a particular course of action is to give a metaphorical interpretation of a set of circumstances. It is my subjective interpretation rather than an objective reality.

To say that God has opened a door for me means that I have perceived an opportunity to serve God (or, at least, to do something that is consistent with my Christian calling). Furthermore, it suggests that circumstances favour the pursuit of this opportunity. The traditional view of doors would encourage us to see the favourable circumstances as a sign that this is God's will.

What, then, are we to make of a missionary who rejects a promising opportunity to preach the gospel merely because his friend is not with him? A bit of a wimp? An unfaithful wretch who ought to be sacked by his mission society? In fact, this is precisely what the apostle Paul did on one occasion! As we have seen, he speaks of an open door in Troas (2 Corinthians 2:12). However, he goes on,

> I still had no peace of mind, because I did not find my brother Titus there. So I said good-bye to them and went on to Macedonia (2:13).

Paul clearly believed that God had arranged the circumstances so that the people of Troas were receptive to the gospel. Yet he did not interpret this God-given opportunity as somehow revealing God's will for him. The opportunity is not necessarily a call.

God may lead me in a particular direction through a particular set of circumstances. That may not be the only reason that an opportunity should stand out to me, however. I may see it as an opportunity because it is what I want to do anyway: it happens to strike me more forcefully because unconscious desires have already sensitized me to it. Alternatively, it may be a way of rationalizing a temptation. I may be attracted to a new job or sphere of service by its material benefits, power over others and all the other worldly reasons and, yet, fail to acknowledge its real attraction. Instead, I delude myself that this is an opportunity to serve Christ more effectively; that it is an open door.

What about closed doors? I decide to do X, but then circumstances conspire against me

Not long ago, we had a striking experience of this sort. We were looking for a larger house because we wanted to develop a ministry of hospitality. We found the ideal house and managed to put together a financial package that would enable us to buy it. That same week, Lawrence heard that he was to lose a job that provided a significant element of his income, making it impossible for us to go ahead with the purchase.

A closed door? We would interpret it in those terms because, just a few weeks later, Di received an unexpected offer of work. If we had committed ourselves to the house and a ministry of hospitality, she would not have been able to pursue this offer. However, that is our interpretation of events rather than a statement of fact. It is equally possible that our sense of a door closing was an overreaction to perfectly ordinary difficulties. Such an overreaction may in fact be evidence of an unconscious unease about a particular course of action.

Hindrances to our plans are not necessarily a sign that God is saying 'No'. It might be that opponents (personal enemies or enemies of the gospel) are hindering the plans. In an illuminating aside near the beginning of his letter to the Romans, Paul reveals that his plans to visit them have been hindered many times (Romans 1:13). Nevertheless, he does not conclude from these difficulties that God does not want him to visit Rome. No, his eagerness to preach in Rome remains undiminished (Romans 1:15).

What, then, are we to make of circumstances?

Contrary to the tradition of open and closed doors, circumstances do not unequivocally show God's will for us. If a particular set of circumstances is pointing towards (or away from) a certain course of action, that is something we should take seriously. This is another piece of data for the process of responsible discernment.

The primary danger with the tendency to look at circumstances in terms of open and closed doors is that it fosters irresponsibility. It tempts us to let God decide for us and notify us of his decisions through our circumstances. As a young Christian looking for a first job, Lawrence took this approach. Fellow CU members advised him that he could rely upon God to make sure that the first job he was offered was the one God wanted him to accept. The effect of such advice was to block any interest in the conditions of the job - if God wanted him to do it, that was good enough. Looking back, this was clearly nothing more than the line of least resistance with a Christian veneer.

Taken to extremes, such reliance on circumstances to guide us slides into fatalism. It means that whatever comes is the will of God. However, as Dallas Willard points out,

> If you wish to know what God would have you do, it is no help at all to be told that whatever comes is his will. For you are precisely in the position of having to decide in some measure what is to come.[4]

In any case, there are strong biblical precedents for suggesting that we should not accept that whatever comes is the will of God. Abraham did not acquiesce in God's decision to destroy Sodom (Genesis 18:16-33). Moses argued with even greater effect against God's decision to destroy Israel (Exodus 32:10). Elijah would not accept the death of a child as God's will (1 Kings 17:20-21). And, as we have already noted, Paul refused to be deflected from his purposes either by hindrances or by God-given opportunities.

If I cannot treat my circumstances as doors that God is opening or closing, how should I approach them? Our account of guidance suggests that a more appropriate way of looking at them is to treat them as data to be interpreted (or discerned) prayerfully.

A friend of ours has described his experience of changing vocational direction in terms which suggested the phrase 'prayerful discernment of circumstances'. Some years ago he was a senior executive in a successful engineering business. However, success was not enough. He had an increasing sense that his job was not fulfilling. Since he was a Christian he devoted much time to prayer and reflection about the matter. Then came the recession. He had a crucial role to play in his firm during this period. There seemed no way out – to leave would be to betray employees and their families. Eventually the firm was taken over, but he continued to work for it.

Some time later, while on a business trip, he visited a project he had been involved in some years earlier. At the time it had been an award winner. Now it was obsolete and in the process of being demolished. That sight struck him so forcibly with the pointlessness of his work that he says, 'God spoke to me on that building-site.'

The following week, the new chairman announced that they needed to cut the senior staff. Our friend's fresh insight into his own position enabled him to assess his circumstances in a very different manner from his colleagues. He realized that he no longer had a crucial role in the firm. In fact, his was the least clearly defined of the senior posts. He also noted that, in contrast to his colleagues, his desk was fairly clear (with no major outstanding projects requiring his attention). These considerations enabled him to accept redundancy and seek an opportunity for Christian service instead. This does not mean that he has become a pastor. On the contrary, he continues to use his managerial skills. However, he now works for a church-related organization.

Extraordinary circumstances

The Bible recounts many occasions when God has guided people in extraordinary or even miraculous ways. However, the consistent teaching of the Christian churches has been that we should respect the unusual character of such events. In other words, while recognizing that God may choose to guide in such ways, we should not seek miracles as a matter of course.

This is not to imply that miracles do not happen. There are many well-attested cases of God guiding through remarkable events or chains of 'coincidences'. For example, Chad Varah describes a remarkable sequence of circumstances surrounding the foundation of the Samaritans. He had the idea for a telephone hotline for potential suicides but was too busy in his parish at Clapham Junction:

> So I said to God, 'Don't look at me. Surely you can see I am busy? This mission to save people from suicide, if it's done at all, will have to be done by one of those parsons who has a church in the City with no parishioners to speak of.'[5]

Shortly after praying that prayer, he received an invitation to apply for the benefice of St Stephen Walbrook in the City of London. When asked what he would do if appointed, he told the patrons of his vision for a telephone hotline. To his surprise they liked the idea and appointed him. The story continues:

On my way to visit the church, I had been pondering about the most appropriate telephone number to ask for, one which would be easily memorized and give a hint of emergency. I knew the exchange would be MAN, short for Mansion House, and I wanted it to sound something like 999, so I hesitated between 9999 and 9000. Eventually I settled on MAN 9000 as being the ideal emergency number on which to get in touch with a man, *i.e.* a fellow human being.

In the vestry, I eventually found the telephone under a pile of broken timber. I lifted it gingerly, as it was covered in dust, and dialled the operator. I asked whether the number could be changed to MAN 9000 and was told that it was most unlikely, since nobody having such a good number would be willing to part with it for love or money.

I mentioned that I had no money but plenty of love and could I please be informed who at present *had* the desired number.

'What number are you speaking from?' enquired the operator.

I replied that the dial was covered with dust, and was tersely advised to wipe it clean. I licked my thumb, cleaned off the centre of the dial, and there it was: MAN 9000. 'Don't worry,' I said to the operator, 'I've got it already.' Then I addressed God: 'Very well. I get the message. You had it waiting for me since the telephone was first installed. Now please stop, because it's getting eerie.[6]

What about fleeces?

The practice of putting out a fleece derives its name from an incident in the book of Judges. Confronted with the terrifying promise that God would use him to free Israel from Midianite domination, Gideon demanded two miraculous signs involving a fleece (Judges 6:36-40). Critics of fleeces sometimes suggest that this is a unique incident. There is, however at least one other biblical account of someone seeking a miraculous sign to confirm God's message (King Hezekiah asked for a shadow to move miraculously in 2 Kings 20:8-11).

These incidents differ in at least two significant respects from the modern practice of putting out a fleece. Both Gideon and Hezekiah requested a clear miracle. And they did so in order to confirm a message that they were already inclined to accept as divine in origin. By contrast, the modern practice seeks an arbitrary event as a divine indicator that something is or is not God's will. It is as if God had lost his voice: 'Nod your head for yes, shake for no.' Garry Friesen confesses to having used fleeces in relation to dating:

> Then there is the 'phone fleece' method of dating. I used to be quite good at it. On those occasions when I did not know which girl the Lord might want me to take out on a particular date, I would set up these 'providential signs' in advance: if no one answered the phone, that meant

God wanted me to call back later; a busy signal was a closed door – I shouldn't call back (maybe some other fellow was asking her out); if she answered but turned me down, then God did not want me to take her out (nor did the girl); if she answered the phone and accepted my invitation, she was the one![7]

Since the events requested as signs are arbitrary, you might as well ask God to influence the toss of a coin: heads you want me to do it, tails you don't. Most Christians would balk at this, but, interestingly, there are far stronger biblical precedents for coin-tossing (or drawing lots) as a technique for seeking God's guidance than for putting out a fleece. However, as we have already noted, such practices introduce an element of impersonality that seems inappropriate when what God desires is a personal relationship with us.

Furthermore, the practice of putting out a fleece is notoriously open to abuse. Writes Adrian Plass, on choosing between carol singing and a James Bond film:

Laid a 'fleece'. If a midget in a Japanese admiral's uniform came to the door at 9.04 precisely, I would know that God wanted me to sing carols. 9.05: A miracle! No-one came. That's that then.[8]

We can bias the outcome of a fleece by laying down more or less stringent conditions for its fulfilment: 'If God does not want me to buy a new car, I shall not see any cars on the way to work this morning.' 'If God wants me to buy a Renault Espace,

I shall see five on the way to work this morning.' And, if the outcome disappoints me, there is always room for negotiation: 'Well, I certainly saw four, and what I thought was a Toyota *might* have been a Renault.'

This is not to suggest, as many writers do, that putting out a fleece is always illegitimate. After all, there are those biblical precedents, and here is an interesting contemporary example.

To appeal against their expulsion from Switzerland, Francis and Edith Schaeffer had to find a permanent home within a matter of days. At the last moment, a chain of surprising circumstances led Edith to a potential home. The difficulty was that it was for sale. They had no money to buy a house and, since they were under threat of expulsion, the very idea was crazy. Under such extreme circumstances, Edith began to pray:

As I asked for God's guidance concerning the chalet which had seemed such an exciting answer to prayer that afternoon and now seemed so impossible, my own logical sequence of thought brought me to begin a sentence in which I expected to ask that the owner change his mind and let it. It was after a length of time during which I had been inwardly struggling for reality in my sincerity of wanting God's will, when I came to this specific request concerning the chalet. It was then that suddenly I became flooded with a surge of assurance that God can do anything, nothing is impossible to Him. My sentence changed in the middle, and I ended my prayer with a definite plea, which even startled me as I asked it, 'Oh, please show us Thy will about this house tomorrow, and if we are to *buy* it, send us a sign that will be clear enough to convince Fran as well as me, send us one thousand dollars before ten o'clock tomorrow morning.'[9]

The next morning, they received one thousand dollars from a couple in America with the proviso 'both of us feel certain that we are meant to send you this money ... to buy a house somewhere that will always be open to young people'.

This was putting out a fleece in the spirit of Gideon: a faithful request for clear confirmation that what seems, humanly speaking, to be utterly crazy is indeed the will of God.

The importance of information

Too often, ignorance blinds us to our circumstances and to the possibilities for service that exist within their confines. Sometimes our circumstances blind us to injustices perpetrated to maintain our privileges. An essential part of the process of seeking God's will is the dispelling of such convenient ignorance by the discipline of being informed.

Being informed involves more than just listening passively to those aspects of the news that the mass media choose to communicate to us. Such news is heavily coloured by all kinds of interests: economic interests, political interests, the broadcasters' awareness that few English people have much interest in, for example, Francophone Africa. The discipline of being informed means actively seeking out alternative sources of information to complement the biases of

103

the mass media. It also means being selective. The modern world is simply too complex for us to be adequately informed about every part of the globe. It would not be beyond the bounds of possibility, nevertheless, for a church to set up regional prayer groups with a particular interest in each continent of the world.

What has being informed to do with seeking God's will? According to the Victorian Christian socialist, clergyman and author of *The Water Babies*, Charles Kingsley, 'A man's eyes can only see what they've learnt to see.' Francis Dewar expands on this by suggesting:

> If we are to be generous with our gifts and energies we need to be well informed, to listen to news, read books and articles, take an interest in current affairs, read newspapers. We need to be aware of how the media slant their reporting and why. We need to have some understanding of people's real needs if our activities are not to be misplaced.[10]

Putting it another way, we need to learn to see the world as God sees it. But, before we can see it as God sees it, we must first look. In an age of global electronic communications, ignorance about the world is tantamount to a refusal to take that first step of looking.

However, it is not enough just to be informed. If we are to see the world through God's eyes, we must turn that information into prayer. In doing so, we are submitting ourselves to a process of sensitization to the real pain of the world.

The need is not the call

We have already made this comment, but it bears repeating. When we perceive a real human need, it is an opportunity for service, not an obligation. An opportunity for service is not, in itself, a call to service.

The complexities of modern life place increasing demands even upon those who are not in the public arena. One busy housewife has neatly summarized these pressures in the following terms.

> Another phone call had come in the middle of breakfast asking if I would do volunteer work at the school one day each week. I had already received requests to cook for a bake sale, be on a phone committee, serve as a room mother, teach Sunday School, and watch a neighbour's child. In addition, yesterday a friend had invited me to go with her to visit a museum. There were too many needs to be met and too many opportunities to take advantage of.[11]

Too often the trite formula 'The need is the call' is used to bypass responsible decision-making. In a simpler and less busy society, a perceived need might be a reasonable indication of a call to service. However, the sheer complexity of our society means that we cannot possibly respond to all the calls to service or take advantage of all the opportunities. How do I choose between a dozen conflicting requests? Do I keep saying 'yes' until I reach saturation-point? Such an approach is irresponsible. On the one hand, it is a recipe for exhaustion and breakdown. On the other hand, it promotes inadequate or half-hearted responses to genuine needs.

We are called to be responsible before God. That may mean not jumping into action at the first sign of a need. Rather, we should take the needs that we perceive as being another important element in the process of decision-making. After all, God may be calling different people to respond to that need in different ways. God may call one person to become a medical missionary. However, for every medical missionary, God may call many people to respond financially. Others may be involved in the administrative and logistic support necessary for missionary work. Yet others will be called to train missionaries theologically and in practical ways. We are not isolated individuals, but part of a body, the church.

Six

Be advised

Beyond individualism

> No man is an *Island*, entire of it self; every man is a piece
> of the *Continent*, a part of the *main*; if a *clod* be washed
> away by the *sea*, *Europe* is the less, as well as if a
> *promontory* were, as well as if a *manor* of thy *friends*
> or of *thine own* were; any man's *death* diminishes *me*,
> because I am involved in *Mankind*; And therefore never
> send to know for whom the *bell* tolls; It tolls for *thee*. [1]

If this is true, our life-decisions are not simply our own
business, to be made in private without consultation.
The modern ideal of total personal freedom, which
has done so much to foster individualism in our culture, was a reaction against tyranny. As with every
reaction, there is a tendency to go too far. Fearful of
domination by others, we have been encouraged to
cut ourselves off from one another.

However, if my decisions affect others, how can I
in good conscience take those decisions without

considering their likely effects on others?

The decision to leave home clearly affects the family as well as the individual. My departure changes the dynamics of the family left behind. Leaving home is therefore stressful for those who stay behind as well as for the one who goes. Similarly, when a couple decide to get married, their decision affects both families. This new relationship changes all their other relationships. Many breakdowns in family relationships may in fact be traced to a refusal to recognize the extent of such changes.

Of course, we cannot base our decisions entirely on what might cause the least disruption to those around us. Far from it! Sometimes God may actually use such disruption to bring new life into a situation that has become closed to his initiatives (hence the South American slogan, 'May the peace of God disturb you'!). This is a reminder that my decisions almost invariably have implications for others.

Even an apparently entirely private decision may have consequences that extend to others. For example, many people would regard watching a pornographic video as a private matter. But is it? That decision has implications for the viewer's attitude to sexuality which may affect his or her personal relationships. It also supports the exploitation of women (and men) by the underworld of the pornographic film-maker.

In reality, I can do little that does not affect others, simply because God created human beings to be social animals. So, when considering a possible course of action, I ought always to bear in mind its likely effects on others.

The fact that my decisions affect other people, however, is not the whole story. If human beings are social animals, creatures made to reflect God in their personal relationships, I am living at a lower level than God intended when I behave as an isolated individual. When I take my decisions without consulting others (and, particularly, without reference to the rest of the body of Christ), I am acting in a less than human way; my decision-making will be incomplete, skewed, perhaps biased in the direction of my own selfish interests. Seeking the advice of others in the decision-making process is not merely a matter of fairness. It is, above all, a matter of trying to function in the way God intended.

Often, sharing the decision-making process with others can shed fresh light on the decision itself. A striking example of this is an experience recounted by an Anglican priest we know. Some years ago he was being considered as a possible incumbent for a large parish in South Africa. He and his family were willing to go if that was where God wanted them. Circumstances seemed to be pointing in that direction. On paper, he seemed the right man for the job.

Before making a final decision, he met with a number of representatives of the parish. It was clear that, as far as they were concerned, this was just a formality. They talked it over and prayed together. To everyone's surprise, by the end of that meeting the consensus was that this would be the wrong move. Shortly afterwards, Nelson Mandela was released from prison and the Apartheid system began to be dismantled. In the light of these dramatically changed circumstances, it would have been quite inappropriate for that parish to have appointed an English priest.

Personal advice

Personal advice is not easily come by in our culture. The breakdown of traditional forms of community has forced more people to turn to experts. Some pay for professional counselling; others turn to computerized services (particularly for careers counselling); yet others opt for more esoteric forms of advice such as astrology; and increasing numbers of people resort to the new army of agony aunts and uncles that is such a feature of the mass media today.

At the root of the problem lies the sharp separation between private and public that is a peculiar feature of modern western culture. Work takes place in an impersonal public sphere that is entirely cut off from the private world of home, church and recreation. Because the public world is seen as more important than the private, its requirements tend to dominate. For example, the increasing mobility demanded by the public sphere hinders the development of stable personal relationships within a community. But, in spite of these pressures, God created human beings to exist in personal relationships, and people invariably find new ways of developing and maintaining such relationships. It may be true that because of mobility (among other factors) our personal relationships tend to be more in number but shallower than those of our ancestors. Nevertheless, they are still relationships and, therefore, essential to fully human decision-making.

It is a worthwhile exercise to make a mental inventory of your personal relationships. With whom do you actually relate in a personal way? This is different from listing all the people in your address book. Many of our relationships (particularly at work) are not fully personal: the secretary, who is treated as little more than a human peripheral for the desktop computer; the woman in the canteen, who might as well be a serving-machine; the cleaner, who is not even noticed. Even in our private lives there may be people whom we would describe as friends or acquaintances but whom we treat as little more than useful instruments. For example, in one of her novels, Susan Howatch portrays the young Nick Darrow as working through a succession of girlfriends for his own selfish gratification. As you think through your personal relationships, other questions you can ask yourself are: Whom do you treat as fully human? Whom do you care for? Whom do you worry about? Your list may include family members (though it may equally well exclude some or all of them!), friends, colleagues (for those who are in work), fellow members of support groups or networks, and so on.

Clearly, seeking the advice of everyone with whom you are personally related on every major issue in your life would be quite impractical. Therefore, before seeking any advice, you must decide whom you will approach. Three criteria are worth bearing in mind.

Advice is likely to be more helpful if the people you ask know you well. Given the complexity of life today and the fact that we know different people in different contexts, this may mean that who you approach will depend on the issue you are considering. Another factor to bear in mind, of course, is that people who know you well may have vested interests in persuading you to decide one way rather than another. Or, they may have blind spots about you (*e.g.* your old Sunday School teacher may be unable to envisage you as a potential pastor or priest simply because of the nature of the former relationship).

It is also worth considering who is most likely to be affected by your decision. How they feel about your plans should certainly be borne in mind. In this case, even more than in the previous case, they are likely to have a preferred outcome, and they may try to persuade you to choose their preferred option.

Finally, there are the people whose opinions you particularly value: men or women whose Christian lives display the kind of maturity you desire; or people whom you recognize as having particular expertise or experience in a specific area. We shall explore this dimension more fully in the final section of this chapter.

However, personal relationships cannot be manufactured at short notice. It is too late to develop a relationship of trust with another person when you urgently need advice on a particular issue. In any case, befriending someone because you want their advice is the wrong motive; and because you are operating from the wrong motives, you run the risk of distorting the relationship from the outset.

As we pointed out earlier, personal relationships are

an integral part of what it is to be human. It is only as we relate to one another personally that we reflect the living God. Therefore, we should be developing our relationships now, not for what we can get out of them (whether advice or security or something else) but simply for their own sake.

Churches could be doing a lot more to help here. They can and should be communities of resistance that consciously oppose the rampant individualism of our culture, and that provide opportunities for us to be more closely related to one another.

Expert advice

Personal advice is clearly important, but this does not mean that you should discount other sources. These range from the quasi-personal (professional counsellors), through questionnaires and computer programs designed to make sense of a bewildering array of data, to books and articles offering expert advice on every subject under the sun.

Even the least personal sources of advice can usefully provide additional information for your decision-making. Take, for example, consumer reports in magazines like *Which?* Such reports compare and contrast the features of a range of commodities (from washing-powders to pension schemes) and make suggestions about best buys. They provide expert advice and enable us to make informed decisions about major purchases. As a result, they ensure that we are better stewards of our money, our time, and possibly also of our environment.

Such advice often seems more objective than personal advice. Objectivity and impersonality should not be confused, however. A major limitation of such reports is that their authors may subtly bias them to favour a particular outcome. Which is the more efficient way of heating a home, electricity or natural gas? The answer may depend on who sponsored the survey!

The above example suggests another limitation. The more impersonal forms of advice are most helpful for relatively impersonal decisions. They work well for consumer decisions. They are also widely applied to the area of career choice – at least, at the stage of narrowing down the range of careers one might be interested in. However, they are of little use in deciding something more personal, *e.g.* whether I should marry this person, or not.

Pastors, shepherds and spiritual directors

Traditionally, church leaders have been treated as sources of wisdom on all manner of things. At one time, the local priest or minister was the most educated man in the village and one whom all kinds of people might approach for advice. In his classic, *The Country Parson*, George Herbert advised would-be ministers to be full of all knowledge (including farming and medicine) that they might be able to minister to all the needs of their parishioners.

Among the forerunners of modern evangelicals, the Puritans took this role particularly seriously, with puritan ministers exercising an influential role as fathers-in-God for the entire community. A similar role was adopted by Charles Simeon who, as vicar of Holy Trinity in Cambridge, became the spiritual father of an entire generation of evangelical clergymen. John Newton exercised a similar ministry through his copious letter-writing, functioning as spiritual director to many influential evangelicals at the end of the eighteenth century.

However, the increasing complexity of our society has compromised this traditional role. In a simple agrarian society, a well-educated man or woman would give good advice on the entire spectrum of possible subjects. That is no longer the case, and the role of spiritual guide or father-in-God has to be adjusted accordingly. In any case, there is no scriptural basis for the popular myth of the omnicompetent pastor. God gives gifts to the entire body of Christ for the good of the body as a whole: there is no suggestion that, as a matter of course, those gifts are concentrated in a single person. Nevertheless, there are some people to whom God gives the gift of being able to relate everything back to the central relationship with God: a gift closely associated with the role of spiritual director.

To modern evangelical ears the phrase 'spiritual director' has a distinctly Roman Catholic ring to it. It conjures up images of being closeted in the confessional with one's priest. Or it may suggest a narrow concern with the interior life of prayer (as, indeed, has been the case until relatively recently in Roman Catholic spirituality). However, a spirituality

115

concerned only with interior spiritual states is no true Christian spirituality.

The liberation theologian, Gustavo Gutiérrez, hit the nail on the head when he wrote:

> The initial encounter with the Lord is the starting point of a *following*, or discipleship. The journeying that ensues is what St Paul calls 'walking according to the Spirit' (Romans 8:4). It is also what we today speak of as a *spirituality*. [2]

Spirituality is about walking according to the Spirit; it is about discipleship. It is therefore about every aspect of my daily life as it relates to God. A spiritual director is one who by example and advice helps me to bring every aspect of my life into relationship with God. When it comes to decision-making, the role of my spiritual director may be to remind me to keep relating the decision to God.

In this connection, we ought to say a word about the phenomenon of 'shepherding'. Shepherding is a system of pastoral care found in some churches whereby every member is put under the authority of a more senior (more mature?) Christian. Like spiritual direction as described above, it relates every aspect of life back to God. There is therefore no no-go area for shepherds: they can direct the financial, social and moral lives of those under them.

In his book *Restoring the Kingdom*, Andrew Walker points out that, as a system, shepherding is particularly open to abuse. At its best, shepherding is akin to spiritual direction as described above. Ideally, a relationship of mutual trust and respect will exist between shepherd and sheep. However, as the term suggests, shepherding is inherently paternalistic. It is assumed that the shepherd's maturity gives him or her authority over every aspect of the sheep's life.

Furthermore, shepherding tends to be part of the formal structure of the church rather than a voluntary arrangement. Anyone belonging to a church which practises it will have a shepherd imposed upon him or her. There is much scope for abuse when the role of spiritual director is confused with the power structures of the church. Of course, this is not limited to shepherding churches. Similar potential for abuse exists in the more traditional hierarchical churches when arrangements for the spiritual direction (usually of clergy in these cases) are integrated into the church's structures for monitoring and disciplining its personnel.

You can avoid such dangers by avoiding such relationships. But to do so is to miss an important aspect of the Christian pilgrimage; and one with particular relevance for the question of divine guidance and decision-making. God did not intend human beings to be isolated individuals answerable only to himself. Christian existence is existence within a community of believers and, therefore, within a network of personal relationships through which we can receive encouragement, support, advice and admonition. You should, however, only enter into a shepherding or spiritual-direction relationship with your eyes open to the risks. In particular, it should satisfy two basic criteria.

To begin with, such a relationship ought to be

117

voluntary. Any attempt to impose a shepherd or spiritual director upon you should be a warning to you to be wary.

Having established such a relationship, both parties should be clear that it is purely advisory. The directee seeks advice of the director. The director (or shepherd) makes, hopefully, sensible suggestions to the directee. However, the director's job is to encourage the directee towards Christian maturity. This will include helping him or her to become more responsible before God. Making decisions for the directee is not a legitimate part of spiritual direction or shepherding. The director should, therefore, allow the directee the freedom to decide before God whether or not to follow the advice. Any attempt to bully the directee into accepting the advice is an unacceptable violation of the directee's God-given personal integrity. This bullying may be quite subtle, insinuating that the directee's standing within the church or degree of Christian maturity depend on following the leader. Or it may be crude and direct: 'This is God's word for you' (implying that this is a direct divine command which you ignore at your peril). There have even been cases of Christians being subjected to exorcism because they have refused to accept the advice of their leaders.

Mutual support

God's priorities are not the world's. If God is a part of our decision-making, he will open for us new ways of looking at the choices we have to make. Indeed, he will present us with new choices. This means that prayerful decision-making will not make for a comfortable life. It leads into conformity with God's will rather than adjustment to the world around us. We become round pegs in square holes or, as a contemporary American theologian has put it, 'resident aliens'.

Making decisions that reflect God's will may bring me into conflict with the secular world. A prayerful decision to follow a particular vocation may seem crazy to non-Christian friends and family. A decision not to co-operate with a company (or government) policy that I feel to be immoral may be regarded as treachery, or it may even be punished as a criminal act.

Given the risks involved in Christian decision-making, therefore, we cannot simply go it alone. We need to be part of a community that shares our commitment to prayerful decision-making. That is one function of the church.

What does this mean in practice? Weekly attendance at public worship will not suffice. Prayerful decision-making needs to be undergirded by mutual support. Genuine, practical support of this sort can be invaluable in several ways.

By now it should be apparent that prayerful decision-making is time-consuming. Yet time is scarce in our culture. The pressures of work and the bewildering variety of leisure-time novelties have steadily eroded the amount of time that is available for decision-making. However, those same pressures have also greatly enlarged the spheres of life in which decision-making is necessary. A mutual-support group can enable us to find the time we need. For example, members of such a group might look after each other's children, allowing couples to get away from the pressures of home and family life for a weekend.

Such a support group is a ready-made pool of personal advice. Different members will have different areas of expertise and can bring different perspectives to bear on one another's questions and choices. By sharing your thoughts about a particular life-choice in such a context, you may find that the decision-making process is enriched.

It will often be appropriate to share one's dreams and desires with the group for their prayer and insights. A friend of ours lives in a Christian community where such mutual support is readily available. She writes:

> I think I sort out the difference between following 'my desires' (which may or may not be of the Spirit) and the nudges of the Holy Spirit by sharing with the Brothers and Sisters. The common witness of the Spirit and general fellowship is a 'sorter-out' of motives.

Finally, an understanding support group that shares your commitment to referring all choices to God can be invaluable when the decision goes against common sense (*i.e.* against socially and culturally respectable sense). If God is calling you to go against the flow, having the support of people who understand and sympathize is very valuable (even if God is not calling them to do the same).

The place of advice

When making a major decision, it is best to seek a range of advice. Different people will approach the question from different perspectives. Relying too much on a single adviser may mean that you risk being misled by that individual's blind spots. It also increases the risk of falling foul of the authoritarian abuse of shepherding or spiritual direction. If you are in a church that requires you to be under the covering of a more senior member, why not seek an independent spiritual director or shepherd as well? Do not put too much reliance on just one person.

When getting a range of advice, however, do not try to get too wide a range. It is a well-known phenomenon that, if you want to get things done, you should keep committees small! The more people you consult, the more likely you are to receive contradictory advice that may leave you more confused and uncertain than before. If you are tempted to ask large numbers (by which we mean more than four or five people) for their advice, you should perhaps ask yourself why. Is this a way of procrastinating? Are you trying to avoid the issue by taking refuge in a confusion of voices? Alternatively, do you already have a preferred outcome, so are you simply looking for people who will agree?

In sharing our questions about guidance with others we should be seeking advice, not easy answers. It is a sign of immaturity to ask for advice if you are hoping that the adviser will relieve you of the responsibility of making the decision. Such dependence on the adviser is a well-known danger in counselling and psychoanalysis; one which any reputable counsellor will go to great lengths to avoid.

Advisers are human. Therefore, they are fallible. Even the most mature Christian leaders (whether they be elders, apostles, bishops or popes) make mistakes. Working in concert does not prevent this happening: committees, synods and councils are no less fallible than their individual members. We would expect a mature Christian leader to be prepared to admit his or her mistakes (and to do so specifically, rather than just in general terms). A refusal to admit mistakes, or a band of followers who regard the leader in question as infallible, are danger signs to be aware of when seeking spiritual advice.

Of course, there are occasions when God chooses to speak very clearly through a particular piece of advice. Precisely this happened to us when we were thinking about getting married. The problem was that marriage seemed to conflict with our vocations: Diana was about to begin training for the Anglican ministry in Nottingham while Lawrence was planning to study theology in Glasgow. Should we get married and, if so, should either or both of us abandon the course on which we were already embarked? Or was this vocational conflict a sign that marriage was ill-advised? Many of our friends were inclined to the latter view. Eventually we took the problem to Diana's vicar. He surprised us by saying that, if we loved each other, we should stop messing around and get married. In his view, the decision about marriage took higher priority than decisions about vocation; that the lesser issues would sort themselves out, if we made up our minds about the major issue. On the basis of that endorsement, we decided to ignore all the reservations and get married. Sure enough, within a month of that decision, all our problems about where we should live and what we should do had sorted themselves out.

Recently, Lawrence met that vicar at a conference and was surprised to discover that he remembered that advice. Apparently it was the only occasion in thirty years of pastoral ministry that he had ever told anyone to get married!

While advice may occasionally take such a striking form, its usual place is alongside the other data that we have surveyed in preceding chapters. Advisers should not decide for us, but they may cast new light on the data, giving us additional insights and information, and helping us to see the issues from a different perspective. Advice from family, friends, colleagues and spiritual leaders is therefore a valuable dimension that we should not neglect in our decision-making.

Seven

Prayerful decision-making

The place of prayer

Prayer is our primary means of communicating with God. Since such communication is vital to the kind of decision-making that we are seeking, prayer must permeate the entire process.

Our data-gathering should be steeped in prayer. The reason for this becomes clear when we consider other human activities that involve data-gathering. What you see depends largely upon what you are looking for. A missionary of our acquaintance once told us that, when he and his wife were working in West Irian in Indonesia, they discovered that the tribes-people could not see photographs: they had to be taught how to relate the marks on the paper to the objects that they represented! Philosophers of science now recognize that there is no such thing as an uninterpreted observation: all information is gathered with the expectation that this (rather than another) type of information will be useful or significant. So the way in which we approach the process of gathering data for a decision will influence the data we see. If we have already unconsciously made up our minds, we will be more sensitive to those data that agree with the decision we want to make: it becomes a process of seeking justification for our decision. Personal biases of various kinds will be reflected in the data we gather and the different weights we put upon different pieces of data. By permeating the entire process with prayer (not just 'baptizing' an essentially secular process with the odd prayer), we are opening it up to God. We are, in effect, inviting God to break into our decision-making processes right from their initial stages and to bring to our attention factors that we might otherwise have overlooked or discounted.

Furthermore, we shall never be able to gather all the data necessary to make a fully-informed decision. In opening the entire process up to God, we are therefore inviting him to ensure that we see sufficient data to make an adequate decision.

If prayer, communication with God, is important even in the preliminary stages of decision-making, it is crucial in the decision itself. Having gathered the data, we must put it together. All kinds of secular decision-making techniques (usually business-oriented and sometimes computerized) are available to help us. However, orthodox Christianity reminds us that our finitude and fallenness undermine all such techniques: we are fallible, so all kinds of personal and social factors may distort our reasoning. Opening the process up to God does not assure infallibility (God does not override our humanity in that way).

Nevertheless, it may help us to decide, albeit according to a different set of criteria than those of the secular world. Christian decision-making is not just an exercise in prudential planning. Major Christian traditions have quite rightly identified it as a spiritual exercise (*e.g.* the spirituality deriving from Ignatius calls it 'discerning the spirits').

Sometimes God indicates very clearly the best way forward. Helen Roseveare's call to serve as a medical missionary in the Congo certainly fell into this category:

Daily I asked the Lord for clear guidance, for a definite word from Himself. One Tuesday in April 1951 I tore off the block calendar in the dining-hall and was puzzled by the text there: 'Repair the house of the Lord' (2 Chronicles 24:4, 34:8) ... I pushed the slip of paper in my pocket and forgot it. On Thursday I received a letter from an old school friend ... She enclosed that same tear-off calendar slip saying that the Lord had urged her to send it to me. Amazed, I went and read carefully through those relevant chapters but still could not see what the Lord was saying to me. On the Friday at morning prayers, the leader of the leprosy crusade of our Mission read that same verse, from that same calendar slip, telling us how the Lord had burdened her through it in special prayer for the Congo, our oldest field in the Mission ... Three times in one week the Lord had spoken. But I did not *want* to hear. Not *Congo*, Lord! ... I want to go to a people who have never yet heard the message of salvation. Congo is an established church, a ministry to Christians.

On Sunday, as I made my way to my own home church, I prayed again earnestly that He would speak so certainly that I could not be mistaken. The vicar read the story of Balaam and his ass (Numbers 22) and he preached on verses 31 to 33! 'Three times the Lord has clearly spoken to you,' he said. 'But you do not want to heed … Heed His voice in His thrice-repeated message and obey – and He will bless.' I went home very soberly, but completely convinced that He would have me to serve in Congo.[1]

God can speak in all kinds of ways. Our part is to listen. His voice will often be less dramatic and directive than in that case. Angela Ashwin cites the following written meditation, in which the author comes to see that God's call is to a hidden support ministry:

I was looking at the pencil in my hand, and thinking about the wood which surrounds the lead. I thought to myself, 'This thin piece of lead wouldn't be much use without the strong wood to hold it. Yet people only seem to be interested in the marks made by the lead, and not in the wood that supports it. So the wood has a hidden role, without which the pencil's drawing and writing would never be possible.' And I wondered if God was asking me to have a hidden ministry too. I can't do much, or make my mark on the world. But I can support other people by my concern and prayer. It was good to realize that this praying of mine is as important to God's work as the wood is to the pencil lead![2]

Angela Ashwin is quick to point out that such

impressions from God cannot be forced. There is no point in trying to generate spiritual meaning from, for example, the contents of my kitchen cupboards! However, I should be alert. If I pray, I should expect God to respond.

Gospel criteria for our decisions

> As the time approached for him to be taken up to heaven, Jesus resolutely set out for Jerusalem (Luke 9:51).

By any normal human standards this was clearly the wrong decision. The disciples knew it was wrong. Peter tried to stop him and was insulted for his pains. Jesus had set his mind on what was plainly a suicidal course of action. In the end they simply decided, with Thomas, 'Let us also go, that we may die with him' (John 11:16b).

The example of Jesus is a warning to everyone who is bent on allowing God to influence their decision-making! We may find ourselves doing things that by the most enlightened worldly standards are simply crazy. Jackie Pullinger sold everything she had and bought a one-way ticket to Hong Kong, arriving with just a few pounds in her pocket and no contacts. Crazy – but it was the beginning of a remarkable ministry to the addicts, prostitutes and gangsters of the Walled City. Repeatedly, God calls men and women to abandon successful careers in order to enter some form of Christian service. Perhaps even crazier, certainly more courageous, are the men and women he calls to remain in their secular careers as his witnesses, prepared to blow the whistle on the injustices and illegalities they see.

Yet if we are not to decide on the basis of worldly criteria, what criteria are we to use? Perhaps the most important is the question of consistency with Scripture: if Scripture clearly contradicts a particular course of action, it is one that Christians will want to avoid (except as a lesser evil).

Closely related to this is the question of conscience. Paul invokes this in relation to eating food sacrificed to idols, advising the Roman Christians to follow their own consciences while trying to avoid scandalizing the conscience of others. Usually, you should not do anything you would feel guilty about doing. On the other hand, neither should you exercise your freedom for its own sake if that would damage the faith of another person.

A third criterion would be consistency with your gifts. The gifts you have been given are a good indicator of what God might expect of you. Yet they are not an absolute guide. God may call and enable you to do things for which you have no natural aptitude.

These are all essentially negative criteria, however. They may be helpful in narrowing down the range of options on which you have to decide, but they give little positive guidance as to which one of a set of options might be the best course of action. Does Scripture give any positive assistance in the decision-making process?

In Deuteronomy 30, Moses challenges the Hebrews in these terms:

> This day I call heaven and earth as witnesses against you
> that I have set before you life and death, blessings and
> curses. Now choose life, so that you and your children
> may live and that you may love the LORD your God, listen
> to his voice and hold fast to him. For the LORD is your life
> (Deuteronomy 30:19–20).

The Old Testament often describes God's blessing in
fairly materialistic terms but here it is clear that more
than physical life is intended. Moses' challenge is to
choose to love and serve God.

This becomes clearer when we compare it with
one of the best-known sayings of Jesus: 'I am the way
and the truth and the life. No-one comes to the Father
except through me' (John 14:6). To choose life –
fullness of life, not merely physical well-being – is to
choose Jesus. He is the positive standard by which all
our possible courses of action can and should be
judged.

One way of doing this is the spiritual tradition of
the imitation of Christ. We set before ourselves the
model of Jesus Christ as we go about our everyday
life, including decision-making. What would Jesus do
in this situation? Which choice would Jesus make?
Countless Christians have found such an approach to
be very helpful but it does have its limitations. It is not
always easy to extrapolate from the relatively simple
choices possible within first-century Hellenistic
Jewish culture to the choices that confront us today.
In any case, Jesus' vocation was not ours: Jesus'
choices were coloured by his understanding of what
God the Father expected of *him*. There was a unique

personal element that we may not extrapolate to other people. We too exist in a personal relationship with God that is not simply a duplicate of his relationship with anyone else. So there may be choices that only we can make: precedents, even exalted precedents, are of limited use in such cases.

Nevertheless, it is possible to detect certain recurring themes in Jesus' decision-making. We may not be called to make the same decisions. But we may profitably apply the same motives and criteria. Perhaps the clearest criterion is that of service:

> For even the Son of Man did not come to be served, but to serve, and to give his life as a ransom for many (Mark 10:45).

Does my decision increase my opportunities for service? Or is it self-serving? Bill Hybels makes the following point:

> Over the years I've found that if a leading promises easy money and fame and perks and toys, I'd better watch out. Prosperity has ruined more people than servant-hood and adversity ever will. On the other hand, I can usually sense that a leading is from the Holy Spirit when it calls me to humble myself, serve somebody, encourage somebody or give something away. Very rarely will the evil one lead us to do those kinds of things.[3]

Hybels' point is well illustrated by the experience of a friend of ours, who received a call to do something smaller and less impressive for God. At the time he was a successful Bible College lecturer. A sense that something was missing from his vocation had been growing upon him gradually. Several months of regular prayer and reflection did nothing to reveal the source of this dissatisfaction. In the end, he prayed for God to send something out of the blue. The result was a letter asking him to consider becoming the vicar of a group of country parishes. In the letter they were described in glowing terms, but the reality was very different. What our friends discovered was a bunch of tiny and demoralized congregations. To make matters worse, it was plain that many of the parishioners were actively hostile to this appointment. Yet, in spite of the danger signs, our friend and his wife had a growing conviction that this was where God wanted them to be! He took the job and, after several years of struggle, is glad to see genuine spiritual and numerical growth in those parishes.

It is important to remember that service does not mean passivity. The powerful often use the rhetoric of servanthood to encourage the rest of us to remain passive. By contrast, Jesus' servanthood was active: it was love in action. Jesus was proactive: he did not simply wait for opportunities to arise. He made opportunities to display God's love in practical service: teaching, healing the sick (even on the Sabbath), denouncing the evils of his day, cleansing the Temple. The religious leaders were so uncomfortable about being served in this way that they crucified him!

Weighing the reasons

We have described Christian decision-making as a

spiritual exercise, but this does not mean that it is irrational!

Having spent some time gathering the data, I should be better able to work out the options open to me. Sometimes, of course, the very nature of the question clearly delimits the options. Should I marry Jane? Yet even in such a clear-cut case, there are more options than appear at first sight. For example, there is the prior question, should I marry at all? Or rather, does marriage seem consistent with my calling from God? Only when I have thought through this prior question should I be exploring the more specific issue.

In other areas of my life, the data-gathering process may throw up new and, perhaps, unexpected options. For example, I may be a school-leaver interested in a career in medicine. A bit of research and the help of a good careers adviser is likely to reveal far more career possibilities in this field than I had originally imagined. Furthermore, it should tell me what additional training I need for each option, the entrance requirements for the relevant courses and where I might go to study.

Making a realistic assessment of the options is an essential part of any decision-making process. One simple way of doing this is to list the points for and against each option. What are its advantages? What are its disadvantages?

To make comparisons between options, creating a checklist of criteria for which you are looking may be helpful. If you are choosing a computer, factors like price, level of after-sales service, ease with which it can be upgraded, and ability to run the required software effectively, will all be important. An interviewer might prepare a comparable checklist of things that he or she is looking for in a candidate for a particular job. In his helpful book *Priorities, Planning and Paperwork*, Peter Brierley of the Christian Research Association gives examples of such checklists for choosing a church, moving an office, interviewing a secretary and balancing the membership of a council or board .

The point is not to reduce decision-making to the essentially mechanical assessment of pros and cons. Rather, it is to clear away the confusion created by a choice between many options when there are several factors to be taken into account. In this way, it may help to achieve a realistic assessment of the advantages and disadvantages before making the decision. It does not relieve you of the responsibility of coming to a final decision.

Examining your feelings

Decision-making is a personal matter, not a mechanical process. As we pointed out earlier, your feelings are relevant to the process of deciding which course of action is right. If you feel uncomfortable about a particular proposal, that is an indicator which should be taken seriously.

Having made an assessment of the reasons for and against each option, the next step is to examine your personal response to each one. This takes time. For example, Margaret Hebblethwaite suggests that she would spend at least a day with each option.

Remember that we are talking about Christian decision-making. The entire process of dwelling upon the options open to you ought to be steeped in prayer. And the effect of that option on your prayer-life is an important factor in discerning the right way forward. It is only too easy for a course of action to make sense, to fill me with excitement and anticipation, and yet for it to be spiritually deadening.

Margaret Hebblethwaite describes this process as follows:

> Suppose I have reasonably adequate information about a proposed job, and am ready to make a discernment. On day one of the discernment I will pray to know the will of God and to follow it. I will then propose to myself: 'I shall take the job.' I make, as fully as I am able, a commitment of my heart to this proposition, even though it is still only an experimental thought and I am not yet committing myself in reality. I offer this hypothetical decision to God in prayer.
>
> I notice how I feel about it in prayer. I live with it through the succeeding day, letting my thoughts come back to it frequently. I observe what it does to me. For example, it may feel immediately right. I may feel consolation. Perhaps I feel a burst of unexpected lightness and confidence; or perhaps it is just a quiet sense of being in a pair of shoes that do not rub. On the other hand, I may feel desolation. The job may feel onerous, like a tedious and rather unnecessary encumberment. Or again, the responses may take a little time to settle down. I may feel initially scared, and afterwards a sense of freedom when I have really brought myself to face the

possibility. Or I may feel initial enthusiasm, that progressively fades. Or I may feel nothing much at all.[4]

You then repeat the procedure for each option in turn, until one option stands out from the others as being the way forward which seems most spiritually fulfilling. If more than one option seems possible on these criteria, you might then decide between them on prudential criteria or personal preference.

Notice that the way in which you pose the question may affect the procedure. If you are faced with multiple options, there is a danger of confusion if you attempt to make direct comparisons between the options. Even if you only appear to have two options, it may be that neither is the right way forward. Consequently, it is best to look at each option and its alternative in turn before moving on to the next option. For example, my employer has offered me a promotion. I have informed myself as fully as possible about the implications of acceptance and refusal (not just the implications for me, but for my family, for the local church in which we are active, and so on). When I come to the stage of discerning between the options, I should not look only at promotion or staying where I am. Both might be wrong. A fuller picture would be revealed by looking at the situation from different angles: being promoted; not being promoted; staying where I am; not staying where I am. The outcome might reveal that I should not be seeking promotion because it is actually time for me to move on from this firm.

The waiting game

> When a man grows aware of a new way in which to serve God, he should carry it around with him secretly, and without uttering it, for nine months, as though he were pregnant with it, and let others know of it only at the end of that time, as though it were a birth.[5]

The Jewish philosopher and mystic, Martin Buber, is here making the point that our dreams (and, particularly, any that point to creative ways of serving God) require a gestation period. Seeking God's will, like bringing dreams to birth, takes time.

This contrasts sharply with our culture's tendency to insist on instant results. Ours is an impatient society. It is in an ungodly hurry to get things done now. Arbitrary deadlines are imposed upon projects. Decisions have to be made quickly, before adequate information can be gathered. We live in a culture fascinated by novelty. Yet how much genuine creativity is to be found in all that novelty? Perhaps in our haste to have something new we force dreams to become plans before they are ready, and so abort them.

God seems to be in much less of a hurry than we are. He took time (often decades) to prepare the great characters of the Bible for their ministries: Abraham was seventy-five when God called him out of Haran (Genesis 12:4); Moses spent years in exile (Exodus 2:21-24); even Jesus was about thirty before embarking on his public ministry (Luke 3:23). This recalls a point made earlier: God's will is more concerned with our gradual maturing as Christians than with whether we marry a particular person or take a particular job.

Christian decision-making takes time. Gathering adequate information for a major life-decision may be time-consuming. The process of discernment described above may take days or weeks to complete. And that decision may only be a stepping-stone on the way to a further decision-making process.

Given the sheer busyness of life in our culture, it may not be possible to find adequate time for such a process in the gaps. One way of solving this problem is to book times for quiet reflection into your diary weeks or months in advance (as we suggested in a different context in chapter 4). We try to set aside one day per month and, from time to time, take a longer retreat together for such purposes.

Dancing to God's tune

The crucial point in the entire process is the decision itself. You have to decide. Part of being human is that God has given us a great deal of responsibility. We may not evade that responsibility by letting someone else decide for us.

What we have described in the preceding chapters is a process that should enable you to come to a responsible decision in a prayerful context. The point of making prayer the context of the entire process is that, in prayer, I am consciously seeking for my will to be aligned with God's will. I am saying, in effect, 'Your will be done.'

Having then made the decision, I must trust that

God has, in fact, answered my prayer for his will to be done in and through my will. Many of the problems associated with knowing and doing God's will really arise at this point. I have decided, but then I may be assailed by doubts. Am I certain this is God's will? (What am I looking for – direct revelation? If so, what price faith?) I really want to do it, so how can it be God's will? (However, if God has really aligned my will with his, this is just what I should expect.) I might let God down. (True, but he will not let me down.)

When doubts assail you at this point, it is worth considering the possibility that they might be temptations: temptations not to commit yourself to the action(s) implied by the decision. If I listen to these doubts, I remain suspended on the edge of doing God's will, wanting to serve God but not taking the risk of actually doing something for fear of getting it wrong. In other words, I become like the unfaithful steward of the parable who would not risk his master's money and so had nothing to show for his master's trust in him.

David Lonsdale entitled his book on discernment, *Dance to the Music of the Spirit*.[6] Dancing is a good metaphor for Christian decision-making (or for seeking to do God's will). You do not learn to dance by standing on the edge of the dance floor listening to the music. It is only as you give yourself up to the music and begin to move with it that you learn. Of course, you make mistakes. Mistakes in seeking God's will are not to be feared. God can use our mistakes far more fruitfully than our inaction.

The image of a dance also reflects the paradoxical

combination of seeking to do God's will and exercising our God-given freedom. God plays the tune. In seeking to do his will, we are giving ourselves up to his music, learning to flow to its rhythms. But dancers are not puppets. Far from it! One mark of a good dancer is precisely a capacity to respond creatively to the music. So it is with God's will: what God expects of us is not blind obedience but the kind of voluntary self-abandonment that creatively interprets the tune he is playing.

Eight

Guidance and the community

The corporate dimension

The modern western world, as we have already seen, has a strong inbuilt bias in favour of individualism. It is only too easy therefore for books on guidance and Christian decision-making to focus exclusively on the individual.

Such a focus, however, is at odds with the biblical emphasis. Both Testaments show quite clearly that seeking and doing God's will is not a matter for individuals alone. Moses' challenge to 'choose life' was not directed to individuals but to the entire Hebrew community. Similarly, most of the books of the New Testament (and, hence, their implicit and explicit teaching about seeking God's will) are addressed not to individual people but to communities of believers.

The issues about which we need to discern God's will extend to the social level of human life. This is reinforced by the fact that New Testament Christianity has as its vision not just the salvation of individuals but the kingdom of God as a whole. Important as individual salvation is, it remains secondary to this essentially social vision.

At every level of human community (family, house-group, church, the wider society) the processes of seeking God's will must be relevant. Because the dynamics of groups change with increasing size, we would naturally expect to see corresponding differences in their decision-making processes.

False trails

Human sinfulness inevitably results in the distortion of corporate Christian decision-making, just as it may bias or distort our individual perceptions of God's will. However, because the consequences for individuals can be potentially devastating (as dramatically shown in the slaughters at Jonestown and Waco), we ought to take particular note of such distortions. They may act as salutary warnings against particular false paths on which we are already embarked. On the other hand, they may offer helpful insights into what a healthier form of corporate decision-making might look like (on the basis that the worst may sometimes be a corruption of the best).

If we are to learn from corporate distortions, we must get past one common error in our churches, the privatization of discernment. Here, the notion of decision-making as a spiritual discipline is limited to personal piety: the process is seen as relevant only to individuals.

At the corporate level, this may therefore lead to

an entirely secular style of decision-making being adopted. The group may invoke God's presence in an opening or closing prayer but, otherwise, the secular world is in charge.

Several of our mainline denominations have adopted a style of decision-making which is strongly influenced by the British style of parliamentary democracy. Accordingly, the Synod, Assembly or Conference sets up committees that produce reports (just like government white papers and green papers); they table and debate motions (admittedly, more politely than in the House of Commons); and they expect lobbying by pressure groups.

Many evangelical organizations and independent churches have adopted a different secular style. They model their decision-making on the business world: the crucial decisions are left to a board of directors, whose word is final and who may or may not consult others before making their decision.

We are not saying that using secular ways of doing things is wrong. But, when a church adopts a secular practice, it ought to keep it under the scrutiny of the gospel: it should remain open to criticism. Synodical government or government by a board of management should therefore not be treated as absolutes. They are merely tools that may have to be adapted in quite radical ways if they are to be of use in what is essentially a spiritual exercise.

When the church or parachurch organization loses sight of the spiritual nature of corporate decision-making, secular approaches may affect its decisions in several ways. For example, pragmatism may supplant principle. This approach is encapsulated by Bismarck, who once described politics as 'the art of the possible'. When the style and methods of secular politics invade the councils of the church, individuals may find themselves having to vote against their own principles in order to achieve a working compromise with opponents.

Alternatively, a small managerial élite (which may be as small as one person – usually, but not always, the minister) may reduce the rest of the congregation to an unscriptural state of passivity. We know of one evangelical parish where the vicar does not permit members of the congregation to decide which Bible study they may attend. In that same parish, a promising evangelistic initiative was stifled because an ordinary member of the congregation suggested it! That may be extreme, but many Christian laypeople have found themselves unable to take significant initiatives *within* the church. It is arguable that the stifling effect of such managerial élites is one reason for the dramatic growth in parachurch organizations over the last century: what they cannot do within the church, resourceful laypeople will find ways of doing in spite of the church!

Perhaps the least pleasant aspect of secular 'respectability' in corporate Christian decision-making is the presence of Machiavellian ecclesiastical politics. Palace revolutions are not uncommon in churches and other Christian organizations. Judging by the pages of the journal *Leadership*, a significant number of American pastors live in fear of being sacked by influential cliques within their congregations.

An alternative to secular methods of decision-making is to extend the prayerful decision-making of one individual so as to apply to the whole group. Such an approach seems to deny that there is such a thing as society, however. It simply does not recognize that groups function differently from individuals. The most common way in which this extension of individual discernment is achieved is by identifying a particular person (or group) as having a hotline to God.

Often this hotline takes the form of direct revelations that bypass the less direct (but more normal) approach to guidance described earlier. In such cases, the prophet or visionary provides the kind of secure foreknowledge that we warned against at the beginning of the book. A very real danger is that the satisfaction of people's desire for security may tempt them to modify or abandon fundamental biblical teaching if it contradicts the new teaching of the prophet.

This is not to suggest that all prophecy is suspect. On the contrary, God can and does speak in this way. However, there are clear scriptural guidelines which we can and should use to discern whether an individual is taking advantage of his or her prophetic ministry. First and foremost, prophecy may neither add to nor subtract from Scripture. Paul makes the point very forcefully when he says, 'even if we or an angel from heaven should preach a gospel other than the one we preached to you, let him be eternally condemned!' (Galatians 1:8). Granted that a specific prophecy does not fall foul of this rule, it should then be tested by those who hear it (1 Corinthians 14:29; 1

John 4:1-3. Prophecy does not have the same authority as Scripture. When someone addresses us in prophetic terms, it is our responsibility to examine what is said critically, asking what, if anything, God is saying to us through these words.

In addition to these clear criteria, it is worth noting that, in the Bible, the role of prophet is often distinct from that of leader. The man or woman with the clearest insight into God's will is frequently not the leader of the community. There are exceptions, of course, such as Moses. But more typical is a relationship like that between David and Nathan: the prophet Nathan appears in 2 Samuel as the adviser and conscience of the king.

However, even if the discernment does take a more conventional form, there is a real danger of authoritarianism. An individual has been singled out as being better able to discern God's will for the community than the rest of us; clearly it would therefore seem that what that individual says in that situation must be acted upon.

Seeking God's will as a community

The decision-making structure of the early church is interesting because it shows one way in which Christianity has adapted to secular styles without abandoning its distinctive features. For everyday decisions the church rapidly evolved a form of government that resembled the power structures of Imperial Rome. Each local church was hierarchically structured with a bishop in ultimate charge. However, at two fundamental points the ordering of the church departed from the cultural norm. The appointment of bishops was a matter for the consensus decision of the congregation. And doctrine was formulated by consensus decisions taken at councils of bishops (the ecumenical councils that produced the historical creeds).

This combination of everyday monarchy and consensus for major decisions gradually disappeared as more emphasis was put on the authority of the bishops. However, the power of consensus decision-making was rediscovered at the period of the Reformation, particularly by the more radical advocates of reform. This became the basis for Anabaptist church government and, later, for Quaker meetings.

It is sometimes suggested that consensus is a counsel of perfection; that any group of people would only agree on the most trivial of matters. However, the history of the Society of Friends suggests otherwise. Take, for example, the Philadelphia Yearly Meeting of 1758. The most contentious item on the agenda was whether Quakers should continue to own slaves. It was hotly debated for several hours during which time the main protagonist for abolition, John Woolman, remained silent. He chose to pray rather than debate. At the end, he briefly stated his belief that slavery offended God. Where a little while before there had been fierce debate, there was now unanimity. They decided not only to abolish slavery within the Society but to make Quakers who were slave-owners reimburse their slaves for their work!

A more carefully worked-out process of group discernment that aimed at consensus or near consensus emerged at the same time among the vanguard of the Counter-Reformation. Indeed, the very formation of the Society of Jesus was the result of a process of group discernment, carried out by Ignatius Loyola and his friends in Rome in 1538–39.

The Spirit in the church

Part of the problem of corporate guidance in western Christianity goes back to a peculiarly western understanding of the relationship between the Holy Spirit and the other persons of the Trinity. This understanding was devised originally to defend the deity of the Holy Spirit against a heretical understanding of the Trinity. Its passive view of the Spirit as the self-effacing spirit of service has tended to downplay the personhood of the Spirit and to subordinate the Spirit to the other persons.

As eastern orthodox theologians have been quick to point out, this view of the Trinity has had devastating implications for the church. By highlighting conformity to Christ, without a corresponding insistence on freedom in the Spirit, it has reinforced a monarchical understanding of church government. On this view, the good Christian will obey what his or her priest or bishop says because the latter are Christ's representatives. There is little sense that the Holy Spirit can make God's will known to the body as a whole. Instead, God's will is channelled through his ordained representatives.

By contrast, the New Testament presents a picture of the Holy Spirit communicating with the gathered congregation. In Acts 13, for example, the Holy Spirit makes it clear that Saul and Barnabas are being called to a particular mission. The passage suggests that their calling came through something fairly direct, such as a prophecy or word of knowledge. What is less clear is whether the Spirit spoke to a prayer meeting of the entire congregation or to a meeting of the leaders who are named in the first verse of Acts 13. The context is important: the communication took place in the middle of an act of worship.

Apparently, the Spirit also communicated in less direct ways. The council of Jerusalem described in Acts 15 is probably an example of the Spirit leading indirectly. It had to deal with an issue which an appeal to the Old Testament could not settle: the unprecedented success of the mission to the Gentiles. How were Gentile converts to be treated? Should they convert to Judaism in order to become Christians? In other words, was Christianity to remain a sect of Judaism or did it have wider implications? An authoritative divine pronouncement, like the call of Saul and Barnabas, would have been effective but it would not have encouraged the church leaders to think through their faith. What we see instead is a process of deduction; they are forced to develop their response from the logic of the incarnation, from the fact of God in human context. However, as their conclusion suggests, they did not see this as entirely their own work. On the contrary, they acknowledge that the guiding activity of the Holy Spirit has undergirded all their deliberations.

How then might a group of Christians seek God's will together?

Gathering and sharing information. The process begins with a period during which the group seeks to amass as much relevant information as possible. This should be shared among the group in as descriptive a way as possible. It is important that every member be aware of all the information on which a decision is to be based. In this way, the group may avoid the danger of one or two individuals using privileged knowledge as a weapon to influence it in a particular direction. We have come across situations, for example, where a minister has used personal information given in confidence as a weapon to affect a group's perceptions of an individual. Our recommendation is that the information be shared in a descriptive way to discourage debating and point-scoring. The point of the exercise is for the group to come to a common mind about what God is saying to them. In such a situation, methods that set one person against another are potentially destructive. It may even be wise to discourage the formation of 'sides' at this stage for the same reason (the danger of division created by the formation of factions).

Prayerful consideration of the cons. When the group is satisfied that sufficient time has been spent examining the information, it will embark upon a period of silent prayer and reflection. During this time each individual will consider the proposal before the group and amass all the reasons against it. There follows a meeting in which all group members share as simply as possible the various reasons against the proposal.

Prayerful consideration of the pros. The group

then repeats the above process for the reasons in favour of the proposal. By separating out the reasons for and against in this way, it is possible to discourage debating.

The decision. When all the reasons for and against the proposal have been explored in this way, it is time to decide. Again, spending some time in private prayer before deciding may be helpful for the group members. Precisely how they arrive at the final decision will depend on the size and nature of the group. A small group of people who know and trust each other may prefer to hear each member's decision and a brief explanation. A larger group may prefer to decide by secret ballot. Either way, the goal is not to achieve a majority but a common mind.

The point of consensus decision-making, of seeking a common mind about what God may be saying, is that it reflects the unity God intended for the church without riding roughshod over individual members. It is a way of decision-making which maintains the unity in diversity suggested by the Christian understanding of human nature (and, indeed, of the character of God).

Seeking God's will as a family

In our own experience, marriage has had a major impact on our freedom to make decisions about our life. Because we are no longer alone, we are no longer at liberty to decide on an individual basis. Decisions affect the whole family, and therefore have to be treated in that light.

For example, a job decision may have implications for housing, schools and friendships. It may also have implications that extend to the local church (if I am an elder, or deacon, or member of the church council, or active in its life in another way). Sometimes these decisions may be quite complex: at one point we found ourselves having to balance educational considerations against housing when deciding between two parishes.

Some of our readers will doubtless assume that decision-making within the family is actually quite straightforward. After all, the husband is the head of the household: he decides, and the wife and children have to abide by his decision. They will argue that this is the clear and unambiguous teaching of the New Testament, and quote such passages as 1 Corinthians 11 and Ephesians 5 in support of their stance.

It is true that these passages speak about the man being the head of the woman, and, in modern English, the head is usually the boss. Hence the assumption that these passages teach that the man has absolute authority within the household. However, the Greek word used for 'head' did not have the same meaning of authority as it does in English. Paul tends to avoid using the language of lordship or power relationships (except in the titular sense in which we speak of Jesus Christ as 'the Lord'). The meaning is therefore not as clear as is sometimes assumed, so we should interpret it in the light of other biblical teaching and Christian beliefs.

One illuminating comparison is with the idea of God the Father as the head of the Trinity. In Latin he is spoken of as the *fons trinitatis*, the fount of the Trinity, the head in the sense of being the source. The Son freely submits to the Father, but there is no sense in which the son is inferior or subordinate to the Father. Furthermore, the voluntary submission of Son to Father clearly does not imply that the Son was merely being passive.

Note also that, if these passages are to be interpreted in terms of lordship, they would have to be read in the light of Jesus' teaching on lordship. The result is a text that, while superficially supporting the conventional marital relationships of a patriarchal society, is actually quite subversive. Christ manifested his lordship in sacrificial service. So if the husband is lord and master, he is such only to the extent that he sacrifices himself for his wife! The result is not a conventional master-slave relationship but one of mutual sacrifice and submission, in which each partner seeks the well-being of the other as a matter of priority.

The general tenor of Scripture and Christian theology suggests that personal relationships should not be thought of primarily in terms of power. To speak of the husband as lord and master is simply not an appropriate way of describing a Christian marriage relationship. Again, we see this in Paul's writings. He speaks about the headship of the man in 1 Corinthians 11, but almost immediately he moves into the language of mutual interdependence. He goes on to extend the idea of mutual interdependence and the priority of love to cover all relationships within the body of Christ. Similarly, in Ephesians 5 he talks about the husband as the head of the wife but immediately he subverts a secular understanding of headship by shifting into the language of love rather than power. The husband *is* the head of the wife. But, in Christian terms, this means that he is her loving servant rather than her overlord.

The process suggested above for community discernment is easily adapted for use in the family. As before, avoiding debate or argument is important; sniping and contradiction of one family member by another should be forbidden. Obviously the time spent praying about the pros and cons and the decision itself should be adapted to the ages and abilities of family members.

However, it is important to let every member of the family speak: parents need to know what their children feel about a particular course of action, even if the children are too young to have a decisive say in the decision-making process. The Rule of St Benedict makes interesting reading at this point (since Benedict modelled his monastic communities upon a family structure with the abbot in the role of father). Esther de Waal points out that the key to the abbot's authority lay in his being obedient to all, which, as she explains, means 'listening to what they desire and advise … The abbot takes advice from all, irrespective of age or status'.[1] By listening and taking account of every individual under his care, he could avoid an authoritarian style.

When the children are young, it will be the duty of the parents to come to a common mind on behalf of the family. However, the goal of family life is not the continued dependence of the children but their maturity. Christian family life should therefore include training in how to make responsible decisions before God. The family council is a valuable part of this process since the openness of the decision-making process gives the children a model that they gradually learn to apply for themselves. At the same time, there has to be increasing opportunity for the children to decide for themselves. Gradually we give them greater and greater responsibility for their spending, choice of clothes, how they use their time, and so on. Our aim will be to ensure that, when the time comes for them to leave home, our children can make prayerful, responsible decisions on their own behalf.

The place of delegation

The process of group discernment described in this chapter is frankly cumbersome and time-consuming. It is designed to force participants to spend some considerable time praying precisely because it is intended for use in connection with the major decisions in the life of a community or family. At the same time, it is an elaborate process so as to protect the community from the danger of being swept along by the private enthusiasms of a persuasive or charismatic individual.

Clearly such an elaborate procedure will not work for most everyday decisions. There are times when it is right and proper to delegate particular decisions or areas of responsibility to a smaller group or an individual.

We used to live in a Christian community that had learned the importance of delegation. They made major community decisions (*e.g.* about welcoming new members) on a consensus basis, but delegated entire areas of community life. So the guest-mistress was responsible for all decisions about community hospitality, while the farm-manager had the final say in anything that affected the livestock or the gardens. The community expected them to consult any members who had an interest in that aspect of community life, but the final decision was theirs.

Many effective Christian ministries operate by sharing out responsibilities among the members of a team in just such a way. Such delegation can also operate very well within the family. For example, we share out the various tasks involved in keeping our home clean. As a family, we have agreed on who should be responsible for which aspects of cleaning. Now people simply get on and do it, without time-consuming complaints about unfairness or attempts to renegotiate responsibilities

That is the point of delegation. If the routine decisions are clearly the responsibility of this individual or that group, time is freed for the community (or family council) to think and pray about bigger issues.

Nine

When God is silent

That dreadful silence

'The eternal silence of these infinite spaces terrifies me.'[1]

Far from being golden, most silence is terrifying. The thinker and mathematician Blaise Pascal was horrified by the early scientific picture of a vast empty universe devoid of God, a universe which no longer declared the glory of God.

We can find silence profoundly disturbing because we are social creatures. God created us for personal relationships with one another and with him. And personal relationships entail communication. It is the absence of the other person that makes the silence disturbing.

Why then do so many Christians find silence to be enriching? The simple answer is that we seek silence not for its own sake but because, freed from the distractions of this world, we may more easily hear God. Religious people prize silence only because it is conducive to closer communion with God.

When we are silent, we expect God to communicate with us in some way. Yet that does not always happen. In the context of seeking guidance, God does not always reveal his will. We free ourselves from distractions but no inner voice comforts us; no text from the Bible (or any other source) jumps out of the page with the force of a direct personal communication. Such silences, silences from which God is absent, are justifiably disturbing. The popular contemporary author Richard Foster recounts such an experience as follows:

By every outward standard things were going well. Publishers wanted me to write for them. Speaking invitations were too numerous and too gracious. Yet through a series of events it seemed clear to me that God wanted me to retreat from public activity. In essence God said, 'Keep quiet!' And so I did. I stopped all public speaking, I stopped all writing and I waited. At the time this began I did not know if I would ever speak or write again – I rather thought I would not. As it turned out, this fast from public life lasted about eighteen months.

I waited in silence. And God was silent too. I joined in the Psalmist's query: 'How long will you hide your face from me?' (Psalm 13:1). The answer I got: nothing. Absolutely nothing! There were no sudden revelations. No penetrating insights. Not even gentle assurances. Nothing.

… At least 'nothing' is how it feels … well, actually there is no feeling at all. It is as if all feelings have gone into hibernation. (You see how I am struggling for the language to describe this experience of abandonment, for words are fragmentary approximations at best, but if you have been there, you understand what I mean).

… It ended finally and simply with gentle assurances that it was time to re-enter the public square.[2]

Perhaps the commonest interpretation of God's silence is that he is somehow displeased with us. This is natural enough. Since we are social animals, silence is one of the worst punishments we can inflict or suffer. It is quite natural to assume that God is not speaking to us because we have sinned in some way. However, there is relatively little biblical support for such an assumption. True, the psalmists seem to assume that the silence of God betokens an unacceptable distance between him and them (*e.g.* Psalm 28:1; 35:22; 83:1). Nevertheless, generally God appears more willing to speak than biblical characters are to listen. Israel turns her back on God but he does not abandon her to her fate. On the contrary, much of the prophetic literature of the Old Testament came into being precisely because God would not be silent in the face of Israel's disobedience. Again and again we hear Isaiah, Jeremiah and others proclaim 'This is what the Lord says' to a people who would rather not hear.

The most striking biblical example of God's silence is that of his dealings with Job. Could there be a clearer contradiction of the idea that God's silence betokens his displeasure? Job was righteous, and the worst part of his suffering was the silence; the not knowing why it was happening. All he knew was that he had done nothing to deserve such punishment.

God may be silent for good reasons, but the god who refuses to speak to us because of our sin is not the God of the Bible. Neither is God silent because of our immaturity. The notion that God tends to speak more clearly to those who are more mature, or holier, is entirely false. It smacks of a spiritual élitism that has no place in a Christianity informed by the Bible.

On the contrary, we might expect someone to speak more often and more explicitly to someone they do not know well. Our experience of marriage is that, as we go along together, we gradually seem to know more clearly what the other is thinking without having to go through a detailed verbal explanation: a glance or a cryptic phrase is enough to convey an entire message. For example, the phrase 'My own, my dearest' means little to outsiders; but, said in a part-icular way, it evokes an important shared experience and speaks volumes about our feelings for certain situations.

God may be saying less to you, not because you have turned your back on him but because he need no longer be explicit. Your thinking has matured. You now tend to weigh up situations by biblical criteria. You are walking in the paths of righteousness. In such circumstances, you are more likely to hear God speak-ing if you should step off the right path (Isaiah 30:21).

Of course, you may choose not to hear what God is saying. Sometimes, when a person complains that God is silent, it is more a case of that person not listening.

On the other hand, there are times of divine silence when we can honestly say that we are open to what

God might say. The above comments suggest that God will have good reasons for such silence.

Finally, there is the silence that *is* golden. This is the silence of intimacy, of communion. At such times, we do not need words: we simply rest in the enjoyment of the other's company.

As you might expect, such silence is very hard to describe in words! It is the kind of silence that sometimes arises between friends or lovers who have grown to know and trust each other implicitly. Such silence is not mere absence of sound. On the contrary, it speaks of a degree of intimacy that cannot be voiced. It is similar in kind to the occasions when we are reduced to silence by the sheer beauty of the world, or by a particularly moving work of art (or play, or piece of music), or, indeed, by bereavement or news of a disaster – all those occasions when mere words are incapable of describing what we are feeling. But all of these are but faint echoes of the silence of communion with God.

Hindrances to hearing

Sometimes the 'silence of God' is due to the deafness of the listener. However, this failure to hear God is not necessarily the result of wilful disobedience. Several other factors may be involved.

Contrary to the philosophical myths of western culture, we are not essentially disembodied spirits who, for whatever reasons, are temporarily resident in physical bodies. The New Age slogan 'We are not physical beings on a spiritual journey, but spiritual beings on a physical journey' has no place in Christian thinking. We are spiritual beings but we are also physical beings: God created us a unity of the physical and the spiritual.

Precisely because the physical and spiritual dimensions of human existence are not separable, we may expect them to interact with each other. Psychological or spiritual factors may have physical side-effects: chronic states of stress or guilt exact a high price in physical well-being. Conversely, physical factors may affect our psychological or even our spiritual well-being.

Take, for example, the case of Elijah in 1 Kings 19. He has just won a tremendous victory against the priests of Baal but is physically and emotionally exhausted. Jezebel's entirely predictable reaction drives him into a state of depression: he wants to die. God does not respond to him at that point. Instead, he lets Elijah sleep and then makes him eat. God addresses the physical factors before speaking to him.

Illness or fatigue may make it difficult for us accurately to discern God's will. They render us less able to pay attention to those aspects of discernment that are our responsibility. A high fever or a splitting headache are not conducive to responsible decision-making!

Similarly, all kinds of psychological and social factors may have a detrimental effect upon our ability to discern God's will.

One obvious social factor is the chronic lack of time that is experienced by people in modern western cultures. As we have stressed in earlier chapters, the process of making a responsible life-decision before God is time-consuming. Where possible we should try to avoid snap decisions. Of course, it is not always possible to find the time that one would like for making a particular decision. Under such circumstances, we can only trust that God will accept and work through the limitations forced upon us.

On the other hand, for some people, the problem may be too much time. Some of us find it hard to decide. We tend to dither. We are always on the lookout for new factors that need to be taken into account. In the face of a personality prone to such vacillation, a definite time-limit on decisions may be a good thing.

Closely related to our chronic lack of time is the busyness of modern life. As a result, many of us suffer high levels of stress. Stress can take its toll on our decision-making abilities. A common phenomenon among chess players illustrates this. They analyse their position carefully and weigh up the pros and cons of each possible move. However, as the clock ticks away, they run the risk of discovering new moves but having too little time to analyse them. Faced with a hard choice between carefully analysed options, time running out, and a new and interesting but unexamined possibility, they sometimes opt for the new move. Those of us with a well-developed intuitive faculty are particularly prone to this temptation to play our hunches when under stress.

Addictions may also distort our capacity to discern God's will. Obviously, powerful drugs are likely to affect our minds. Yet there are many more subtle addictions to which human beings are prone. We may be workaholics; giving our work an unrealistically high priority and skewing our perception of what God might want of us accordingly. All kinds of things may be addictive. For example, we know of a parish that was split down the middle because many of its members were too attached to an old vicarage set in acres of secluded grounds: they were quite unable to see that not only was it badly located but that it gave entirely the wrong message about the church to non-churchgoers.

Another important psychological hindrance to hearing God is rigidity. Lack of imagination or fear may make us take refuge in unquestioning obedience to certain ideologies or dogmas. So God is only permitted to speak in certain ways or about certain things. We do not permit him to challenge the comfortable myths of our society or church.

Disobedience and deafness

The rigidity that restricts God to certain ways of doing things has a bearing upon one major way in which we allow our sinfulness to filter out what God might be saying to us. In a famous passage, Augustine gives a clear example of how this filter operates:

> I had prayed to you for chastity and said 'Give me chastity and continence, but not yet.' For I was afraid that you would answer my prayer at once and cure me too soon of the disease of lust, which I wanted satisfied, not quelled.[3]

Augustine is uncompromisingly honest about a

tendency that we all share. I want God to be Lord of my life, but I also want to retain control of this area or that area, at least for the time being. So I tend to bracket out certain aspects of the Bible's teaching. I may, for example, take a very hard line on sexual impropriety (unlike Augustine) while conveniently overlooking what it has to say about social justice. Every individual is different and, therefore, will have different blind spots, and different areas of resistance to God's will.

Another way in which we may prevent ourselves hearing what God is trying to say is by deliberately disobeying the clear commands of God. This is, perhaps, more likely to happen with guidance about specifics than about God's revealed will. However, otherwise apparently mature Christians can some- times display a remarkable capacity to reinterpret or rationalize away the clear commands of Scripture if they do not fit in with our will.

In such circumstances, the continued seeking of guidance may be a strategy for avoiding God's will. It is as if we were hoping that God would change his mind. Take the example of Jonah.

'What do you want me to do today, Lord?'

'I want you to go to Nineveh and warn the people that I am displeased with them.'

'You can't mean that, Lord. The Ninevites are the natural enemies of Israel. You really want them destroyed, don't you? This must be a test. You want me to come to a mature rational decision about what I should do. I know – I'll set sail for Spain!'

So Jonah stopped listening to what God was asking

165

of him, but God did not stop speaking. In circumstances such as these, God may even adopt a dramatic course of action to get his message through to his errant servants. In Jonah's case, it was a storm and a great fish.

God's reasons for silence

There are, of course, a variety of situations in which God might have very good reasons for not revealing to us what we want to know and what we should be doing. In this section, we shall examine four such reasons.

Times of testing

As the story of Job suggests, one major reason God might be silent (as opposed to us being deaf) is that he has chosen to test us. Such desert experiences are a treasured part of Christian spirituality. In the early church there were those who sought them out literally, embracing a life of prayer in the desert. Far from being escapist (a peculiarly modern criticism), they firmly believed that they were taking the spiritual battle into the very strongholds of the enemy. The mystic and poet John of the Cross spoke of it as 'the dark night of the soul'. Here is a contemporary example:

> I made my home in an alpine cabin for two months. I
> wanted to spend time with God. To my dismay the
> silence was empty. Even the most familiar comforts of
> faith and assurance were missing. It was a wilderness and
> I had no way of knowing how far it would stretch before

me. I wept over God's absence. I protested and got very angry. I hammered on the walls of the cabin demanding his presence. This was a crisis of faith. How could I believe any more? Who was God anyway? And then I began to realize the nature of my demands. To my crying, 'Who are you?', the silence echoed, 'Who are *you*?' The temptation to negotiate with God runs so deep … God is gift. He cannot be commanded. Up there in that alpine cabin one morning, there came a tearful and profound moment. Kneeling on the wooden floor I told God I would no longer treat him as if I owned him. Life was for him to give and for him to take away. The only claim we have upon him is his love. I confessed the possessiveness that I called 'love for God'. I confessed my attempts to control and dominate. I 'let him go'. I asked for the life that was his gift alone. Something died that day – and something was born. Quietly and surely, spring broke through the death of winter.[4]

Such times of testing are never arbitrary. God does not 'abandon' one of his children out of idle curiosity as to his or her reaction. They are times of testing in the sense of proving or improving. God may use such times to reveal things about ourselves or about God that we could not otherwise come to grips with. In the above example, what was revealed was an insight into the author's attitude to God. In the story of Job, the outcome was a new and awesome vision of God the Creator. For those who experience such times, they may later be seen as crucial stepping-stones in their Christian pilgrimage.

David Runcorn has pointed out that desert

experiences may bear fruit in several different ways. The desert may be a place of *purification*; a place where the non-essentials are stripped away (this is how Richard Foster subsequently interpreted the experience described earlier). The desert may also be a place of *struggle*. In biblical and early Christian imagery, it is the place of the devil. Jesus went into the wilderness at the beginning of his ministry to confront the devil and defeat the temptation to pursue his ministry in more attractive but, ultimately, less fruitful ways (Matthew 4:1-11). The desert fathers went into the desert specifically to engage in intercessory prayer and spiritual warfare against the principalities and powers that held sway over the late Roman Empire. Then again, the desert may be a place for *waiting*. Modern men and women do not like to wait. We are an impatient people. Sometimes God forces us to wait precisely because it is only through such waiting that we can hear his still small voice. Finally, he speaks of the desert as a place of *adoration*: a place where we abandon ourselves 'before the wonder and beauty of God in all his glory'.[5]

Delegating responsibility

Another reason that God might remain silent on a particular issue is that he is allowing you the responsibility of choosing for yourself.

It may be that there is no divinely preferred course of action; that all the possibilities before us are equally acceptable to God. In such cases, whatever you choose to do will be right.

Alternatively, and more commonly, one or more of the options open to you will clearly be better than the others when judged by the criteria described in chapter 7. In situations like these, rather than direct your attention inescapably to the best option, God may give you the responsibility of making the decision for yourself. Here the choice you make becomes a reflection of your maturity as a Christian. As Dallas Willard suggests:

> With respect to many events in our future, God's will is that *we* should determine what will happen. What the child does when not told what to do is the final indicator of what and who that child is. And so it is for us and our heavenly Father.[6]

Finally, it is possible that there is only one right course of action, and that you are in a situation where you should be capable of discerning for yourself what to do without recourse from God. For example, you do not need specific guidance from God about whether or not to indulge in an extramarital affair. That is simply not a legitimate option. If you are honest with yourself, there is no need to ask God's advice on the matter.

The story of Balaam in Numbers 22 is a stark example of this last type of situation. In response to Balak's request for Balaam to go ahead and put a curse on the Israelites, God tells him unequivocally not to go. However, when Balak's messengers return with the same request sweetened with the offer of a handsome reward, Balaam again seeks God's will. Did he really think that God might have changed his mind? Or did the money persuade him to hope for such a change of mind? In spite of supernatural intervention, Balaam maintains his desire to go with the messengers. God acquiesces, and uses the situation to turn the tables on Balak. Nevertheless, Balaam is clearly doing his own will rather than God's.

One step at a time

Another reason for experiencing divine silence when I seek guidance is that I simply do not need to know. The Christian pilgrimage is a walk of faith. I am called to follow Jesus one step at a time. It is not a package tour with prearranged itineraries that I can buy into.

God does not satisfy my idle curiosity about what lies ahead. Sometimes this can be very hard to live with especially if, like us, you like life to be organized and under control. As we write this chapter, we are coming to the end of over a year of uncertainty about our middle-term future. During that time we have had to make various decisions, and we have been confronted by circumstances to which we have had to adapt. Yet there has been no sense of a pattern to these events. We find such untidiness very frustrating and highly stressful. Now, however, it looks as if those apparently chaotic frustrations have conspired together to enable us to respond in a particular way to a particular set of circumstances that we could not have foreseen even a month ago!

It is a bit like climbing a mountain. You want to get to the summit. Yet most of the time, following a straight path from base camp to your destination is impossible. You have to cast around for handholds and footholds. You may have to traverse halfway round the mountain to find a suitable route upwards. Sometimes you may even have to descend some way to reach a point from which you can ascend further. A detailed examination of a small part of the route may not give any clues as to your ultimate destination.

Sometimes God's guidance is like that. As you live through the situation, it is seemingly chaotic or arbitrary. There does not seem to be any reason to it. However, looking back from a later vantage-point, you can see that those apparently meaningless moves enabled you to get where you now are.

Ignorance is bliss

Finally, there are some things that I simply could not handle if I knew about them in advance. I do not yet have the strength to deal with them.

One of the characteristics of God's dealings with his people is his gentleness. Isaiah says of the Servant of the Lord, whom Matthew identifies with Jesus:

> A bruised reed he will not break,
> and a smouldering wick he will not snuff out.
> In faithfulness he will bring forth justice.
>
> (Isaiah 42:3)

God does not impose upon his people any burdens that they are not yet capable of bearing. Sometimes guidance in the sense of foreknowledge would be too much for us to bear.

Handling silence

The silence or absence of God is, quite properly, very disturbing for Christians. Human beings were not meant to exist in isolation from God. The right response, when you become conscious of such a situation, is serious self-examination.

This does not mean that you should indulge in morbid introspection. It is not a matter of assuming that there must be some unconfessed sin lurking deep in your soul. It is certainly not a matter of dredging around for something, anything, with which you can accuse yourself. Self-examination means an honest look at yourself, not indulgence in the kind of self-accusation typical of the 're-education' of Mao's China.

In fact, such self-examination is a traditional part of many Christian spiritual traditions. We meet it in the Jesuit Examen of Conscience. It was part of the Anglican tradition of preparation for Holy Communion: a tradition that could have unexpected, dramatic results, for example the conversion of a dissolute young Cambridge undergraduate in Holy Week 1779. Charles Simeon went on to exercise a preaching ministry in Cambridge for over half a century, during which time he influenced countless undergraduates and others.

Many aids to self-examination exist in print.[7] Often they consist of pointed or challenging questions that shed light on various aspects of your private life. In the context of the silence or absence of God, you might like to focus on whether any of the factors mentioned earlier in this chapter are applicable to you.

172

Are there any physical, psychological or social hindrances to discerning God's will about which you can do something? Perhaps the pressures of your job mean that you are chronically tired. If so, one way of preparing for a major decision might be to take a holiday.

Are there areas of your life that you are withholding from God? Are there practices in your life that you know to be wrong, or about which you feel guilty? Sometimes we need help to see these. This is where a pastor or other mature Christian may be a great help. They may see things we are hiding from ourselves. Nevertheless, we should never accept their assessment of us uncritically. Remember Job's friends, wise men who gave Job a considerable amount of good advice that turned out to have entirely missed the point! As you become aware of sins in your life, they should be confessed. But beware of tying yourself in knots whilst looking for imaginary sins!

Are there specific things that God has clearly told you to do? If so, do them. God is gracious, and will often continue to guide us in spite of repeated failures to follow his guidance. However, it is hardly reasonable to expect guidance when we fail to do what he has already clearly told us. Lest you should misunderstand, this is not a matter of being obedient in order to manipulate God in any way. Rather, it is an integral part of seeking to be as open to God's prompting as possible.

Finally, there are the factors you cannot change. You may be unconscious of them. All you can do with them is to become aware that they exist: that you are finite and therefore fallible. Part of the process of praying through a decision is offering that decision to God in its fallibility, asking God to use even your mistakes to his greater glory, and trusting him to honour such a prayer.

After all this, I may still find myself in a situation where the right way forward is not clear. How should I proceed in such a case? The temptation is to stand still, like the wise hill-walker caught in fog. However, this response assumes the absence of the guide. God may be silent but he is never truly absent. Since a stationary object cannot be guided anywhere, a better response is to proceed with caution, taking care to judge the available options by the criteria we have described earlier.

Ten

No second best

Confirming our decisions

Our western culture places a premium on being right. Truth is not valued because it is true, but because it gives us power. It began with science: Bacon taught us that 'Knowledge is power.' Truth was sought, not because we wanted to enjoy God's thoughts after him but because we wanted to enjoy mastery over nature.

Gradually that attitude to truth has poisoned the western world, just as its rivers and seas are polluted. The thinker Friedrich Nietzsche was the first to point out how far the poison had spread. Today, many academics are cynical about claims that something is true, because they suspect that underneath the truth-claim there is a hidden assertion of power. By contrast, politicians are reluctant to admit that their opinions might not be completely and unequivocally true. Their refusal to admit the possibility of error stems from the same source: they are afraid that such an admission would be an admission of weakness, that it would undermine their power over others.

A similar attitude on the part of church leaders is a sure sign that we have imbibed one of the less acceptable facets of the world in which we live. However, the beauty of the gospel is that we no longer have to labour under the burden of being right. The church is meant to be a fellowship of saints, *i.e.* sinners who have been overtaken by the saving reality of Jesus Christ. To admit our mistakes (and, for that matter, our premeditated sins) is not an admission of weakness but an acknowledgment of our humanity. We can make mistakes, and we do make them.

Precisely because I am fallible, I should not expect that any decision I make will be the end of the guidance process. Such a conclusion would only make sense if I believed that divine guidance offers me infallibility. But, in reality, I cannot know all the implications of a decision until I have begun to live with it. I may have made a mistake. So, while the decision itself may be the crucial point of a decision-making process, it cannot be the end of the matter.

Realizing that this was the case, Ignatius insisted that every prayerful decision should be followed by a process of seeking God's confirmation. As a modern paraphrase of his *Spiritual Exercises* puts it:

> Even after proceeding according to the circumstances outlined above, I will take the decision which I have reached by these approaches and beg God our Lord to accept and confirm it if it is for his greater service and glory.[1]

But what constitutes confirmation that I have made

the right decision? Some Christians point to the biblical concept of blessing. They suggest that God will bless those with whom he is pleased. Some go still further, arguing that in the Old Testament blessing was something quite concrete, resulting in tangible effects like large herds and good harvests. Such Christians may therefore interpret material blessings as confirmation that they are walking in God's will.

However, the cultural context of this interpretation raises serious questions about its validity. It is a distinctively North American approach to blessing. America, the flag-bearer of modernity, is perhaps the most pragmatic culture in the world. For our purposes, pragmatism may be seen as a secularization of Jesus' dictum, 'By their fruits you shall know them' (see Matthew 7:20). In other words, 'If it works, it must be right.'

The advocates of prosperity theology claim that God indicates his approval of their activities by blessing them with health, wealth and happiness. Conversely, sickness, disability and poverty are signs of God's displeasure. If a Christian is materially successful, that is seen as God's blessing on an obedient life. Similarly, if a Christian venture is successful, that is read as evidence that it was God's will.

Such an outlook, however, can lead to the philosophy that the end justifies the means. One prominent American evangelist recently ran a postal fund-raising campaign to finance missionary work among Jews. His organization sent letters to Christians, appealing for specific sums of money so that evangelistic literature could be sent to named Israeli citizens. The letters suggested that, if you failed to respond, you would be responsible for those persons' eternal damnation! Generating guilt may be a successful way of raising money, but what does that success tell us about the will of God?

Such an approach is morally abhorrent. It praises the rich while condemning many heroes and heroines of the Christian faith.

Take, for example, Emily King. Who? That's the point! She was a pioneer missionary in western China, but she did not live long enough to become the subject of a missionary biography. After a brief spell in China, she died of typhus, leaving her husband to care for a five-week-old baby. Little health and prosperity in her experience! What was worth this sacrifice? On her deathbed she cited the eighteen Chinese women who had become Christians through her witness as being her treasure in heaven. Yet, by the criteria of the prosperity gospel, she was a failure.

A prosperity gospel cannot accommodate self-sacrifice or martyrdom. By its criteria, even Jesus himself was a failure, since the outcome of his ministry could hardly be measured in health, wealth and happiness (either for himself or his disciples). In short, conformity to God's will cannot be measured by material criteria. A prosperity gospel is a heresy that owes more to Mammon than to Christ.

If material blessings are not an infallible confirmation that we are doing God's will, how can we know that we have made the right decision?

Sometimes God graciously confirms our decisions in dramatic ways. This happened to some friends of ours (we shall call them Frank and Irene) when they decided to get married. They had agonized over the decision for some time. In the end, Frank popped the question. But, even at this stage, he had nagging doubts. A few days later, he visited a friend with whom he often prayed. This friend knew nothing of what had been going on between Frank and Irene. However, he suddenly asked, 'Have you ever thought of getting married?' Frank admitted that he had, in fact, just asked Irene to marry him. To this, his friend's response was to say, 'In that case, I can tell you that I've been praying about your future. I asked God whether you had any future in this parish and his reply was "None – apart from Irene."'

More often, confirmation of our decisions is less definite: a gradual process as the implications of the decision unfold, rather than a clear-cut word of confirmation. Another friend of ours has never found the seeking of God's will an easy matter. Reflecting on the major decisions of her life to date, she commented that all but one had involved her in doing something she really did not want to do. She described her attitude as resignation to courses of action that were clearly God's will for her, rather than glad acceptance. Yet, in each case, she has found that what began as resignation has been transformed into glad acceptance as she has faced life in the wake of the decision. Her misgivings had been replaced by peace.

Christianity promises its followers spiritual fruit rather than material success. In seeking confirmation of my decision, I should not look primarily at the

179

material blessings that might have accrued. Instead, I should ask whether and how, as I have lived out that decision, I have grown as a Christian. That growth may be inward (the development of my spiritual life) or it may be outward (in greater opportunities for service).

The biblical analogy of fruit should warn us against seeking instant results. Fruit takes time to develop and mature. We have several fruit-trees in our back garden. In the winter and early spring, as we look at them day by day, we see little change. Gradually, over a period of months, we see buds turning into blossom. The blossom withers and leaves behind tiny apples and pears. At last, in the autumn, the fruit is ripe. The growth of spiritual fruit is longer and slower, a process that lasts for years rather than months. Of course this does not rule out the possibility of growth spurts, but these are the exception rather than the rule.

From the perspective of guidance, one of the most important aspects of the fruit of the Spirit is peace (see Galatians 5:22–23). We have already highlighted it as a significant element in the decision-making process: lack of peace about a particular option is a clear indicator that it bears closer scrutiny. Similarly, peace (or lack of it) plays a significant part in the process of seeking God's confirmation.

Hopefully, having made the decision, I will find that I am at peace about it. But sometimes my uncertainty does not diminish after I have made my choice. Alternatively, the act of making the choice may result in a merely temporary release of tension and dispersal of uncertainty: I am content at first, but gradually, as the weeks and months pass, I become increasingly uncomfortable. If this increasing tension and dis-ease seem to be a consequence of my decision, I would do well to reassess it.

This is not to suggest that lack of peace is an infallible indicator that I have made a mistake. Far from it! Our own experience suggests the contrary. After about a year of marriage, we were inclined to think that it had been the most appalling mistake. More than a decade further on, we are now inclined to think that it was one of the best decisions we ever made. The lack of peace, the tension and the dis-comfort were certainly indicators that we should reassess our situation. They pointed to aspects of our relationship that we had to work on together. But they did not indicate that we had made a mistake in getting married.

God's flexible purposes

Some traditional models of guidance effectively deny God's sovereignty. They suggest that God has a unique, perfect plan for each of our lives that we have to discern and follow. This view denies God's sover-eignty because it suggests that, if we fail to discern God's will correctly, we condemn ourselves to a second (or third) best and, by implication, thwart God's purpose for our lives. If this were a realistic model of guidance and if we were honest with ourselves, most of us would have to admit that we are living out God's nth best for us (where n is a very large number, not unrelated to the number of times we have disobeyed God since we were born)!

The Bible clearly teaches that God is sovereign: his purposes will be fulfilled. However, it also teaches that God works through his creation and, in particular, through human freedom.

If I maintain that God has a detailed blueprint for every aspect of our lives, I am forced to adopt an outlook of extreme determinism. In other words, I must believe that, in reality, God has determined everything and our freedom is only apparent. It is very close to fatalism: whatever will be, will be because God has willed it. Forty-eight years ago, on the Feast of the Transfiguration, the allies detonated an atomic bomb above the Roman Catholic cathedral in Hiroshima while worshippers were attending mass. As we write, thousands of Christians are suffering starvation, disease and persecution because of the civil war in Rwanda. According to this extreme determinism, these and all the other atrocities of our century (the killing-fields of Cambodia, the Nazi holocaust, the Turkish Armenocide, for example) are integral parts of God's blueprint for the world!

The alternative is to say that God has a definite outcome in mind and his ultimate purpose will not be thwarted, whatever happens. God's omnipotence is expressed, not as a power that forces every aspect of nature into line, but as an infinite flexibility that can take every situation and redirect it towards his ulti-mate goal. This does not imply that God is not interested in the details, merely that he does not predetermine them. On this view, the horrors of Auschwitz and Hiroshima were definitely not part of

God's will. However, he can take such extremes of evil, suffering and destruction and bring good out of them.

No second best

The Christian life is a pilgrimage, but the blueprint model of guidance effectively turns our pilgrimage into a tightrope walk; a choice of getting it precisely right or disastrously wrong. As a result, we may be tempted to stay where we are. Because the alternatives are presented so starkly, we may feel that ducking the major decision is better than getting it wrong.

The difficulty with this solution is that refusal to decide is itself a decision! What is more, it is the same kind of decision as was made by the unfruitful servant in the parable of the talents. A decision not to move may be a decision not to follow Christ. As John White says:

> You can't follow Christ if you stand still. It is often better
> to make a mistake than not to move at all.[2]

Learning to follow Christ is like learning to walk. It is not something we can expect to do perfectly overnight. We begin by crawling or shuffling along. Gradually we gain the confidence to get up on our feet and take a few steps. Soon we stumble. But we learn by our mistakes.

God's flexibility means that our mistakes do not condemn us to a second-rate or third-rate Christian existence. Indeed, if the blueprint model were correct, not only our own mistakes but those of others might be sufficient to condemn me to God's second best. Instead, we envisage a situation in which his purposes for our lives may change in response to our decisions (right or wrong) and, indeed, in response to the decisions of others.

Talk of God's best (or second best, or nth best) for our lives is simply not appropriate, because it presupposes an underlying blueprint that, if what we are saying is correct, simply does not exist. God's best for our lives is that we should be doing his will right now. No Christian who is walking faithfully in Christ's footsteps right now is living a second-best Christian existence.

Calvin puts our situation beautifully:

> Those bound by the yoke of the law are like servants assigned certain tasks for each day by their masters. These servants think they have accomplished nothing, and dare not appear before their masters unless they have fulfilled the exact measure of their tasks. But sons, who are more generously and candidly treated by their fathers, do not hesitate to offer them incomplete and half-done and even defective works, trusting that their obedience and readiness of mind will be accepted by their fathers, even though they have not quite achieved what their fathers intended. Such children ought we to be, firmly trusting that our services will be approved by our most merciful Father, however small, rude, and imperfect these may be.[3]

Many parents, ourselves included, adorn the walls of their homes and workplaces with works of art created by their children. This is not usually done

184

because of the artistic merit of the work! Rather, the giving and the receiving (which means displaying) of the picture is an expression of the love between parent and child.

In all our decisions, our attitude should be that of the beloved child rather than the anxious servant. What matters is that we offer our decision-making and its fruits to God in an attitude of 'obedience and readiness of mind'. And God, our loving Father, will work with us through the decision and beyond, because he loves us.

Notes

1. The shepherd and his sheep

1. D. Willard, *In Search of Guidance: Developing a Conversational Relationship with God* (San Francisco: HarperCollins, 1993), p. 204.
2. G. Friesen, *Decision Making and the Will of God: A Biblical Alternative to the Traditional View* (Portland, OR: Multnomah Press, 1980), p. 203.
3. Cited by J. I. Packer, *Knowing God* (London: Hodder & Stoughton, 1973), p. 264.

2. The foundations of guidance

1. D. Willard, *In Search of Guidance: Developing a Conversational Relationship with God* (San Francisco: HarperCollins, 1993), p. 68.
2. Thomas à Kempis, *The Imitation of Christ*, tr. E. M. Blaiklock (London: Hodder & Stoughton, 1979), 3.6.2.
3. J. Calvin, *Institutes of the Christian Religion*, tr.

F. L. Battles (Philadelphia: Westminster Press, 1960), III.xx.43.

4. J. Pullinger, *Chasing the Dragon* (London: Hodder & Stoughton, 1980), p. 31.

5. L. Newbigin, *Unfinished Agenda* (Edinburgh: St Andrew Press, 1993), pp. 110f.

3. The Bible and guidance

1. W. Hybels, *Too Busy Not to Pray: Slowing Down to be With God* (Leicester: IVP, 1989), p. 134.

2. Cited by P. Adam, *Guidance*, Grove Spirituality Series No. 27 (Nottingham: Grove Books, 1988), p. 17.

3. Cited by E. Bethge, *Dietrich Bonhoeffer: A Biography* (London: Collins, 1970), p. 560.

4. E. Schaeffer, *L'Abri*, expanded edition (Wheaton, IL: Crossway Books, 1992), p. 76.

5. Cited by D. Tidball, *How Does God Guide? Finding God's Will for Your Life* (London: Marshall Pickering, 1990), p. 103.

4. Know yourself

1. Cited by R. Parker, *Healing Dreams: Their Power and Purpose in your Spiritual Life* (London: Triangle, 1993), p. 80.

2. For more information about the Myers Briggs Type Indicator, see the article in the *New Dictionary of Christian Ethics and Pastoral Theology* (Leicester: IVP, 1995), pp. 616f., or our book, *God's Diverse People: Personality and the Christian Life* (London: Daybreak/DLT, 1991).

3. J. White, *The Fight* (Leicester: IVP, 1977), p. 162.

4. Cited by L. Ryken, *Work and Leisure in Christian Perspective* (Leicester: IVP, 1989), p. 144.

5. A brief but helpful introduction to the idea of quiet days and retreats is John Pearce's *Advance by Retreat: Using Silence to Come Closer to God*, Grove Spirituality Series No. 29 (Nottingham: Grove Books, 1989). Alternatively, you might try the chapter on solitude in Richard Foster's *Celebration of Discipline* (London: Hodder & Stoughton, 1984), pp. 137–155. For more detail on how to make use of such times, Brother Ramon's *Deeper Into God* (London: Marshall, Morgan & Scott, 1987) is an excellent handbook.

6. For a modern evangelical perspective, see Russ Parker's *Healing Dreams*.

7. G. MacDonald, *Ordering Your Private World* (Crowborough: Highland Books, 1987), p. 128.

8. White, *The Fight*, p. 22.

9. H. Roseveare, *Give Me This Mountain* (1966), reprinted in Christian Classics series (Leicester: IVP, 1995), p. 36.

10. *St Ignatius' Own Story*, tr. W. J. Young (Chicago: Loyola University Press, 1980), p. 10.

5. Circumstantial evidence

1. J. Bronowski, *The Ascent of Man* (London: BBC, 1973), p. 432.

2. J. Eareckson, *Joni* (Glasgow: Pickering & Inglis, 1978), p. 142.

3. R. Bauckham, *Freedom to Choose*, Grove Spir-

ituality Series No. 39 (Nottingham: Grove Books, 1991), p. 10.

4. D. Willard, *In Search of Guidance: Developing a Conversational Relationship with God* (San Francisco: HarperCollins 1993), p. 56.

5. C. Varah, 'Phone Call From on High', *Church Times*, 10 April 1992.

6. *Ibid.*

7. G. Friesen, *Decision Making and the Will of God: A Biblical Alternative to the Traditional View* (Portland, OR: Multnomah Press, 1980), p. 125.

8. A. Plass, *The Sacred Diary of Adrian Plass (aged 37¾)*, Basingstoke: Marshall Pickering, 1987), p. 7.

9. E. Schaeffer, *L'Abri*, expanded edition (Wheaton, IL: Crossway Books, 1992), pp. 96f.

10. F. Dewar, *Live For a Change: Discovering and Using Your Gifts* (London: DLT, 1988), p. 100.

11. S. A. Yates, *And Then I Had Kids: Encouragement for Mothers of Young Children* (Brentwood, TN; Wolgemuth & Hyatt, 1988), p. 53.

6. Be advised

1. John Donne, *Meditation*, XVII.

2. G. Gutiérrez, *We Drink from our own Wells* (Maryknoll, NY: Orbis, 1984), p. 54.

7. Prayerful decision-making

1. H. Roseveare, *Give Me This Mountain* (1966), reprinted in Christian Classics series (Leicester: IVP, 1995), pp. 65f.

2. A. Ashwin, *Patterns Not Padlocks: For Parents and All Busy People* (Guildford: Eagle, 1992), p. 46.

3. W. Hybels, *Too Busy Not to Pray: Slowing Down to be With God* (Leicester: IVP, 1989), p. 137.

4. M. Hebblethwaite, *Finding God in All Things* (London: Fount, 1987), p. 209.

5. M. Buber, *Ten Rungs* (New York: Schocken Books, 1947), p. 74.

6. D. Lonsdale, *Dance to the Music of the Spirit* (London: DLT, 1992).

8. Guidance and the community

1. E. de Waal, *Seeking God: The Way of St Benedict* (London: Fount, 1984), p. 138.

9. When God is silent

1. B. Paschal, *Pensées*, iii.206.

2. R. Foster, *Prayer: Finding the Heart's True Home* (London: Hodder & Stoughton, 1992), p. 21.

3. Augustine, *Confessions*, VIII.7.

4. D. Runcorn, *Space for God: Silence and Solitude in the Christian Life* (London: DLT, 1990), pp. 68f.

5. D. Runcorn, *Silence* (Nottingham: Grove Books, 1986), p. 11.

6. D. Willard, *In Search of Guidance: Developing a Conversational Relationship with God* (San Francisco: HarperCollins, 1993), p. 56.

7. For aids to spiritual self-examination, see, for example, Margaret Hebblethwaite's *Finding God in All Things* (London: Fount, 1987), pp. 130–166, or Mark Link's *You: Prayer for Beginners and*

Those Who Have Forgotten How (Allen, TX: Argus Communications, 1976), pp. 111–125. Both of these authors base their material on the Examen of Conscience found in Ignatius' *Spiritual Exercises*. An alternative form of self-examination, based on the fruit of the Spirit as listed in Galatians 5:22–23, is William Purcell's *The Plain Man Looks At Himself* (Glasgow: Fontana, 1962). One that Lawrence has found particularly helpful over the years is Michael Griffiths' *Take My Life* (London: IVF, 1967).

10. No second best

1. D. Fleming, *Modern Spiritual Exercises: A Contemporary Reading of the Spiritual Exercises of St Ignatius* (Garden City, NY: Image Books, 1978), p. 72. (This is based on Ignatius, *Spiritual Exercises,* no. 188.)
2. J. White, *The Fight* (Leicester: IVP, 1977), p. 171.
3. J. Calvin, *Institutes of the Christian Religion*, tr. F. L. Battles (Philadelphia: Westminster Press, 1960), III.xix.5.

Your Guide to Guidance

MARTIN & ELIZABETH
GOLDSMITH

- Choosing a job?
- Considering marriage?
- Facing a major decision?

Your guide to guidance is packed with good
advice that makes sense of the different ways
God guides today: the Bible, wisdom,
circumstances, inner peace and much more.
Find out what it takes to get the right guidance
and how to make decisions in the will of God.

*Martin and Elizabeth Goldsmith live in
Hertfordshire, England where they lecture at All
Nations Christian College.*

96 pages   *Pocketbook*

Frameworks